Ditching Mr. Wrong

NICHOLAS ARETAKIS

Ditching
Mr. Wrong

How to End a Bad Relationship
and Find Mr. Right

next stage press

Published by

Next Stage Press, LLC,

24950 N. 107th Place Scottsdale, AZ 85255

480-220-3700

www.DitchingMrWrong.com

ISBN-10: 0-9776224-3-6

ISBN-13: 978-0-9776224-3-6

Book design by Alicia Mikles

Manufactured in the United States of America

Library of Congress Cataloging-in-Publication Data is available

This book is dedicated to the millions of women each year searching for Mr. Right.

Contents

Preface

THIS BOOK IS DEDICATED TO all the single women out there who are struggling to find that special someone. In today's frenetic society, women must juggle their personal, professional, and financial goals with the quest to find their life's companion. With so much going on, they often find themselves compromising, spending months or even years with men who aren't worth their time.

The search for a mate should not be taken lightly. Choosing the right man is one of the most important decisions you will ever make. Your happiness and lineage depend on it.

Ditching Mr. Wrong provides a series of simple tests, exercises, and pieces of advice for women to implement as they sort through prospects. The book profiles twenty characteristic male personalities, with guidance on how to determine whether a man may emerge as a good husband, father, provider, friend, and partner for life. Most women will quickly recognize the man in their life in one or more of the profiles.

The objective of *Ditching Mr. Wrong* is not to help you score a weekend fling or choose someone entertaining to bring to the office holiday party. This book won't help you find someone who looks good on your shoulder. This book will help you identify a quality male partner who is worth your precious time. And your time is precious, especially if you want to have children.

I want to help women accelerate the recruitment process. They should not waste valuable years of their single life in low-quality relationships when they can move on to better possibilities.

Ditching Mr. Wrong is not about proving that all men are bad. Quite the contrary. It's about helping women hone their mate selection skills and keep poor candidates from dominating their schedules and their lives. *Ditching Mr. Wrong* provides sage advice on how to get rid of a guy who doesn't have the tools to be a lifelong partner, at least not for you. It's about quickly getting back in the dating game and finding someone who fits your requisite qualifications.

Relationships between men and women are challenging enough, but the wrong man will inevitably lead you to an unhappy life. Learn to identify Mr. Wrong quickly and dispose of him properly, preventing negative emotional and financial long-term effects. It's not as hard as you think, especially when you see that *Ditching Mr. Wrong* is not really about how to break up with someone. It's about moving more quickly toward your ultimate goal: finding Mr. Right.

Introduction

WOULDN'T IT BE GREAT IF, after going on a few dates with a guy you thought was a great catch, you could take a pill before bedtime and wake up the next morning knowing for sure whether he was Mr. Right or Mr. Wrong? How about a truth serum that would make him completely honest and forthright during early courtship? These magic potions would save a lot of time and mental anguish. If the results were unfavorable, you'd be able to get you on your way toward identifying other prospects.

I wish such magic existed, but there's no way to make finding a life partner that easy.

But I can help. After I got married, I found myself increasingly intrigued by the dilemma so many of my wife's girlfriends and other women I met faced. They wanted and deserved to find the right guy to settle down with, but ended up dating guys—for months or even years—who were clearly wrong for them.

As an entrepreneur and a seasoned executive in the technology field, I'm analytical by nature and believe that most problems, when viewed objectively, have effective solutions. I have interviewed hundreds of women. I've observed plenty of flawed couples in my social and professional circles, and have met others on my extensive travels. I've gathered additional stories of romantic disappointments from third-party experts who counsel women on relationship issues. All of these women have one thing in common: They want nothing more than to avoid wasting valuable time on the wrong guy.

What I have learned from their tales of failed relationships is that *it actually isn't very hard to identify Mr. Wrong.*

You need only a few basic tools. First, you need a way to look at your current partner *objectively*, as if you were evaluating a relationship between two strangers. I offer several ways to assess a man, including the all-important *Dating Litmus Test,* a thorough measure of gauging the quality of your relationship.

Then, you need to be able to increase your dating savvy by getting acquainted with the twenty most common types of Mr. Wrong on the singles scene today. I've developed these profiles after recognizing certain behavioral patterns and attributes in the guys the women I interviewed described. Each profile identifies warning signs you can spot *much sooner than you think,* with guidance on when to ditch a guy and when there's hope for the relationship.

Ditching Mr. Wrong doesn't stop there, of course. You'll need to know how to end the relationship you may now realize isn't right, and then how to get back into the dating game, this time with your Mr. Wrong detection skills finely honed.

My goal here is not just to help you find the right guy. I want to help you build a lasting, quality relationship. I want fewer women to think, after those wasted months or years (or decades!), "I wish I'd known better." I want more happy couples out there. I want more children growing up in homes in which their parents are devoted to them *and* to each other.

Another reason for this book is to prevent the singles scene from being contaminated with what I call the *dating virus*, when the impact of one individual's bad behavior is passed from relationship to relationship. For example, if a woman's latest romance soured because the man cheated, she may anticipate the next guy she dates will act the same way. Her suspicion may undermine the potential of the new relationship, stifling it before it can evolve. The man in turn will worry that *his* next candidate will doubt his fidelity just like his last girlfriend did, burdening his efforts to find love. This kind of *negative response behavior* spreads the dating virus far and wide, making for a rather downtrodden assortment of eligible men and women. I hope to help women realize that they don't need to put up with the misdeeds of Mr. Wrong. The sooner they ditch him, the more likely it is that their attitude toward future prospects won't be ruined.

And, frankly, I'm bothered by the guys I see getting away with treating women poorly. I'm no saint, mind you. I didn't get married until I was forty-two, and I thoroughly enjoyed being single. Obviously, I had relationships that didn't last, but I think my exes would all call me a good guy, just not *the* guy. What I'm talking about are the guys I've known and heard about who've lied to, deceived, cheated on, abused, and even stolen from the women who loved them. And many of these were women with all the right stuff—smart, successful, attractive, and nice.

I realize some men might think I'm betraying The Secret Handshake, that covert knowledge about guys that's supposed to stay between guys. Some men may have contempt for my profiles of Mr. Wrong, finding them inflammatory, derogatory, or stereotypical. Some men have told me what I'm doing isn't fair. Aren't there plenty of Ms. Wrongs out there too?

I'm not stating all women are perfect. But I do want to say that women have much more at stake in learning how to get rid of the wrong partner and find the right one. If they want to have children, there's a deadline. After the age of thirty-five, their chances of conceiving and having a healthy baby begin to plummet. By their mid-forties their fertile years will come to an end, with little hope even for those who can afford the financial, emotional, and physical cost of the latest high-stakes fertility treatments.

This deadline didn't used to be as much of an issue, because people married earlier. Today, young adults are putting off marriage, quite often into their late twenties, thirties, or beyond. It's one of the many aspects of adulthood they are delaying. Young adults are taking longer to graduate from college, find a career, live on their own, and break financial ties to their parents.

There are plenty of pitfalls to postponing entry into the "real world," as I discuss in my book *No More Ramen: The 20-something's real world survival guide* (www.NoMoreRamenOnline.com). In the case of delayed marriage, women suffer the drawbacks more than men, who can and do sire children far later in life (some well into their sixties). Whatever you may think of these grandpa dads, the reality is that the male biological clock doesn't tick nearly as loudly.

Women who want to bear children have to take control of their lives and their relationships, especially if they are approaching thirty and don't have any children. I call this period the dating *danger zone*. This is the time when many women realize they have to get serious about finding the right man, even though many of their unsuspecting male contemporaries may have no idea why these women are worrying about the future.

But planning ahead is incredibly important. Let's analyze why, using the following simple mathematical model:

Timetable to Land a Man

✳ SIX MONTHS TO THREE YEARS
to find the right person

✳ SIX MONTHS TO THREE YEARS
to have a productive relationship

✳ SIX MONTHS TO A YEAR
to plan a wedding

✳ A YEAR OR TWO
of marriage to ensure a good fit and
enjoy "newlywed" status

✳ ONE TO THREE YEARS OR MORE
(if there are infertility or other medical issues)
to start a family

That makes the minimum time from single status to motherhood approximately *three and a half years!*

The medium amount of time (a more realistic gauge) ranges from *five to seven years.* The process often takes over *ten years.* For a woman now thirty, that means waiting until her late thirties or early forties—a late age—to have a child. A second one may not be an option.

Now let's contrast this with the less urgent situation of the man. He may theoretically like the idea of being married one day, but for him the issue of when that day comes isn't as urgent. Men have the luxury of being more self-centered, putting work and friends ahead of a finding a Mrs. They may be enjoying an extended adolescence. In my bachelor days, I used to joke that marriage was always within five years, but *time zero* was the variable. In other words, the (open-ended) five-year clock would start when I realized I was ready for a wife, and I didn't really know when that would be.

Something just short of the perfect storm must occur to make most men ready for marriage, with at least some of the following factors falling into place:

He's Truly Ready for Marriage When...

✳ He meets his match, physically, intellectually, and emotionally.

✳ He feels he's ready to settle down.

✳ His professional and personal objectives overlap with his intended wife's.

✳ He feels marriage won't distract him from his educational path (or he's completed his education and requisite training).

✳ His career is stable.

✳ He wants to have children.

✳ He can afford it (the wedding, a home, the cost of raising a family).

✳ He's tired of playing the field.

It's a tall order, especially when men have plenty of time to fill it.

The good news is women can exponentially improve their chance of finding Mr. Right if they can accurately assess their compatibility with a man and take the time to learn how to spot Mr. Wrong.

Let me tell you about one of the women I interviewed. Her story is one of the driving forces behind this book's publication. She's a nice woman and a close friend of my wife. She dated a man for several years who cheated on her, bought a house with her money, and told elaborate lies to cover for his sins.

That horror story took a lot to recover from, and unfortunately it wasn't the only major romantic disappointment in her life. But eager to change her pattern of falling for Mr. Wrong, she read excerpts from this book as I wrote it and is becoming one of my best test pilots. My wife and I got a phone call recently, all about the new guy in her life she proudly...dumped. As much as we'd love to get the good news that she's finally found the right special someone, we're thrilled that she has resolved not to waste any more time.

"I'm getting better," she said. "This time I ditched him sooner."

She's on her way. And now that you've decided to learn about Mr. Wrong, so are you.

The Top Ten Mistakes Single Women Make

✳ Dating a guy for superficial reasons, such as looks, money, or popularity

✳ Making an early decision to commit to a guy before really getting to know him

✳ Spending more time on less important pursuits, such as major purchases or where to live or work, than on the quest to find a lifelong partner and potential father for her children

✳ Focusing her personal life completely on a relationship, meanwhile letting go of her own social network and support group

✳ Removing herself from exposure to more viable prospects too early in a relationship

✳ Staying in a bad relationship far too long, ignoring the early warning signs

✳ Compromising career and personal goals to accommodate her man

✳ Trying to change him

✳ Hitting the "baby panic" (or the "lonely panic") button and settling for far less than she deserves in a significant other

✳ Losing her sense of independence and self-esteem

PART ONE

Are You Dating Mr. Wrong?

First Impressions: It's Never Too Early to Ditch Mr. Wrong

THE FABLED FIRST DATE! WHETHER it's the traditional dinner-and-a-movie, a walk in the park, or a trip to an amusement park, the first date is often a time when hopes and fantasies can blind you to reality. You can get so enthralled with the idea of a man's interest in you that you may fail to learn much about him.

It's important to enjoy yourself on a first date, but don't get lost in a fairy tale. I like to classify the first date as the *résumé date*. You should use the occasion to screen prospects as intently as you would for a critical hire at your workplace. You actually should scrutinize him with even more care. This guy may end up in bed with you, or even have access to your finances!

The Résumé Date Checklist

✳ Compute a background check to see whether you know anyone in common.

✳ Make a mental note of the length and present status of past relationships.

✳ Is he emotionally damaged from a past relationship?

✳ Learn what he does for a living, and how successful he is.

✳ Get a handle on his earnings capability and professional stature.

✳ Determine whether he has a sense of humor.

✳ Find out who his friends are. Are they the type of people you would like to be associated with?

✳ Does he have "baggage," such as children, alimony, dependent relatives, pets, debt, or pending litigation?

✳ What are his overall likes and dislikes?

✳ Is he a positive person, one who sees the glass as always half full?

No matter your hopes, fantasies, or level of physical attraction, you should process what you learn with objectivity. Discoveries that make you uncomfortable may mean a first date should not lead to a second. Why waste your time?

Often, the biggest clues about whether you're out with Mr. Wrong come not from what you learn about him, but from how he treats you. Women will often overlook bad behavior from the moment they meet a man, just because something about him catches her fancy. But these first impressions are crucial. Men should be on their *best* behavior at this point. If your date's efforts don't fulfill *The First Date Bill of Rights*, his treatment of you probably won't get any better.

The First Date
Bill of Rights

✳ *Reliable:* Did he call you when he stated he would?

✳ *Accessible:* Did he provide you with his cell phone number and e-mail address, in case you need to reach him about an unexpected change in plans?

✳ *Approachable:* Did he welcome you to contact him at any time?

✳ *Conscientious:* Is the planned activity both convenient and enjoyable?

✳ *Accommodating:* Did he suggest and book a suitable place to meet?

✳ *Thorough:* Were you impressed with the arrangements that were made?

✳ *Polite:* Did he show good manners?

✳ *Connectable:* Was it easy to talk, or did making conversation feel like "pulling teeth"?

✳ *Attentive:* Did he listen to what you told him or hinted about your personal preferences?

✳ *Generous:* Did he reserve a table at a restaurant suitable for intimate dialogue, and did he tip appropriately?

✳ *Comfortable:* Did you leave with the feeling that you would really enjoy spending time together in the future?

✳ *Chemistry:* Are you physically attracted to your date?

✳ *Integrity:* Did he seem honest?

✳ *Safety:* Did you feel secure throughout the evening?

If he falls far short in any or several of these categories (one or two small deficiencies may be excusable), starting a relationship with him may not be a good idea. Don't despair—you're now free to look for other, better candidates.

If all goes well, a first date may lead to another, then another, and you're off on the Road to a Relationship. But don't speed down this road in a souped-up convertible with the top down, irrespective of much fun it seems to be! Keep your eyes open and your judgment intact.

Don't ignore signs of what I call *relationship deal breakers*. These are qualities, habits, and attributes you just know you can't live with. Deal breakers vary from woman to woman. You may not mind a man who smokes, for example, but your best friend could never tolerate it. *Know your own deal breakers* and check for them as early as possible in the guy who's caught your interest.

Top Twenty Relationship Deal Breakers

✳ *No Prime Time:* He's always busy on Friday and Saturday nights.

✳ *Nothing in Common:* He's a sports enthusiast, you live for the ballet, and there's no middle ground.

✳ *Family Matters:* He always has major family obligations or faces significant issues in his family, such as interpersonal strife, mental illness, disease, a disability, or a disorder.

✳ *Religious Differences:* Can you face the possibility of compromising or converting? Can you agree on how to raise children, if desired?

✳ *Politics:* You fundamentally disagree on candidates and ideology.

✳ *Obsessions:* He's a workaholic, an incessant trainer, and a fanatical enthusiast, and these obsessions take up all his time and mental energy.

✳ *Bad Habits:* He is a slave to cigarettes, drinks excessively, smokes pot regularly, or abuses harder street drugs or prescription medication.

✳ *History of Bad Habits:* A man "in recovery" could relapse.

✳ *Loner:* He has no close friends from home, work, college, high school, team sports, or even the bar scene.

✳ *Jealousy:* If he doesn't trust you, particularly around other men, it often means that he doesn't trust himself.

✳ *Rudeness:* He's impolite to strangers, co-workers, friends, family, or people in the service industry.

✳ *Poor Hygiene:* He has bad breath, body odor, or other forms of poor hygiene.

✳ *Poor Health:* He doesn't take care of himself and is often ill or tired.

✳ *Unemployed or Underemployed:* He doesn't work very often, very hard, or at all.

✳ *Idle Rich:* He's a trust fund baby who seems to have no responsibilities and lacks a value system.

✳ *Values:* He has moral standards you can't abide, such as his views on abortion or whether a woman should leave the workforce to raise children.

✳ *Lost:* He doesn't know his purpose or have any direction.

✳ *Boring:* Your mind wanders when it's his turn to speak.

✳ *Aesthetically Unpleasing:* You find him physically unattractive.

✳ *Hothead:* He has a short fuse and possibly a "chip on his shoulder."

As you assess your early compatibility, remember that a relationship with a man will always feel at least a little bit like visiting another planet. *Men are from Mars, Women are from Venus*, remember?

They don't call men and women "opposite sexes" for nothing. They tend to act differently— at times, *very* differently. Accepting the vast gender divide can be crucial to approaching the dating game with wisdom and humor.

Here are just a few examples of the different ways women (*W*) and men (*M*) tend to see the world (and each other):

The Gender Divide

Cell phone usage:

W: dial-out, mostly for receiving voice mail or text messaging

M: bilateral use and typically an appendage of the body

Returning e-mails and phone calls:

W: delay so as not to appear overeager, following *The Rules*

M: whenever they want, or when convenient

TV remote sleep timer:

W: don't usually know how to use or even locate

M: standard operating procedure after ten p.m.

Movies about sports, violence, westerns, or slapstick comedy:

W: remotely interested, never repeat viewing, prefer a magazine

M: will watch over and over, in part or entirety, reciting key parts

Retail shopping:

W: for fun and bonding with friends, taking their time, browsing

M: out of necessity, typically alone, highly focused speed shopping

Dining out:

W: will never finish all the food on their plate

M: will clean their plate, then take aim at their date's

Personal grooming:

W: haircut, color, style, manicures, pedicures

M: haircut only when absolutely required

Doctor visits:

W: on a regular basis

M: emergency basis only

Home cleaning services:

W: tidy up prior to house cleaner arriving to avoid sloppy appearance

M: won't clean up for weeks prior, avoiding even routine maintenance

Pillow talk/bedroom manner/carnal activities:

W: foreplay, sex, talk, hopefully more sex

M: foreplay, sex, uninterrupted sleep

Dressing:

W: looks and style

M: warmth and comfort

Constructive feedback on a woman's comment, "Does this dress make me look fat?"

W: thinks "yes," but says, "it's not flattering to your figure"

M: thinks "your ass makes you look fat," but states, "it looks okay"

Time required to get ready for a night out:

W: one hour minimum

M: five to fifteen minutes

Driving:

W: defensively

M: offensively

Online dating:

W: love, companionship, long-term prospects

M: quick candidates, weekend date, short-term rewards

Exercise:

W: get in shape or remain fit, work to squeeze into one-size-smaller outfits, alternative social network

M: relieving competitive juices, bonding with the boys, staying in relative shape

Dancing:

W: dance to the rhythm of the song

M: move to the voices in their head

Decorating abode:

W: monthly, quarterly, or spontaneously

M: move-in and move-out dates

Changing the sheets:

W: weekly or after having guests

M: after someone points out that the top and bottom sheet stick together

Washing towels:

W: every other usage

M: every other month

Decorative pillows:

W: requisite for home décor

M: what are decorative pillows?

Shoe inventory:

W: one pair for each day of the year

M: one pair for each day of the week

Purchasing:

W: buy in bulk, thinking only of future requirements

M: buy as needed, thinking only of now

Don't let these differences frustrate you. You can be perfectly compatible with a man who doesn't act or even think the same way you do all the time. Remember, you're not looking for a best girlfriend. You're looking for a male partner and, potentially, the father of your future children.

Second Impressions: Are You with the Right Guy?

I F YOU'RE ALREADY IN A relationship with someone, you need to ask: Are you with the right guy? The most important step in ditching Mr. Wrong is to take an unflinching look at your current partnership, with as much objectivity as you can muster.

It's not an easy thing to do! I spoke with Gretchen Sunderland (http://www.coachgretchen.com), a life coach, about why women don't acknowledge fatal flaws in their relationships. She pointed out a stark difference between male and female attitudes on courtship:

> "Women make up their minds early in a romantic relationship and won't easily change their opinions or plans once they decide that they want to remain with or even marry a particular man."

Women often get locked into the idea of the *potential* of a prospect, instead of evaluating who he is now. During the courting process, which could be months or even years, she finds ways to excuse her man for his shortcomings.

She'll rationalize them away, deflecting criticism from close friends and family. Or she will assume that, with her help and love, he will change. However open-minded, generous, or kind this assumption may seem on the surface, it's simply misguided. True personal transformation is rare, especially once a man has entered his thirties.

Instead of waiting forever for their man to change, women need to ask themselves one crucial question:

"Would I start a serious relationship with my present significant other if I knew everything about him that I know today?"

If your answer is "no" or "I don't know," you need to put your relationship to the test. Literally. Even if you answer "yes," you may still be in defensive, "stand by your man" mode and need further evidence of the health (or lack thereof) of your relationship.

The following Dating Litmus Test will help you evaluate the man you are with, not the man you hope to be with. It's important to be perfectly honest in your answers. Proceed as if *no one will see these results but you.* Be introspective, and don't bias yourself by taking the test after a rare fight with your partner, or when you're depressed about work or other life circumstances that aren't directly related to him.

I recommend that you take the test no sooner than three months or ten dates into a relationship, whichever comes first. Before that point, you can use the test questions as a guide for what you need to find out as you get to know your new man, but don't score him yet. Remember, *The Résumé Date Checklist, The First Date Bill of Rights,* and the *Top Twenty Relationship Deal Breakers* should help you weed out poor prospects.

The Dating Litmus Test

For each question, answer as honestly as possible, assigning one of the following scores to each answer.

0 = Definitely no!
1 = Probably no
2 = Uncertain (or does not apply)
3 = Probably yes
4 = Definitely yes!

Add up your numbers, and see the bottom for your final score. Remember, you are not grading yourself. Your final score will give you an indication of how your boyfriend ranks as a prospective life partner. It's helpful to take the test more than once (hide earlier results until after you have retaken the test to avoid biasing yourself). If you haven't known your partner for much longer than three months or ten dates, you may not be able to answer some of the questions. If you are in the first weeks of a relationship, there are some questions that will (and should) remain uncertain, such as whether he wants to have children. Give him a "2" on the questions you can't answer yet, and take the test again in a few months to compare results.

A downloadable copy of the test is available at (http://www.DitchingMrWrong.com).

Dating Litmus Test

1. Do you look forward to seeing him when you've been apart?

2. Do you find your partner entertaining and interesting?

3. Do you share similar interests, usually agreeing on how to spend time together?

4. Do you find more things to appreciate and respect in your partner as time goes on?

5. Do you have an enjoyable sex life, one that is satisfying physically and emotionally? Does it make you feel good to please him?

6. Are you physically, intellectually, and emotionally attracted to him?

7. Does he make you feel better about yourself? Has your confidence or self-esteem improved during your relationship?

8. Does he pay attention when you speak and truly listen?

9. Is he considerate of your feelings and desires?

10. Do you trust him, rather than feeling the need to check up on him to make sure he's not being dishonest or cheating on you?

11. Can he be counted on to make the right decisions about his finances or professional life?

12. Do you have compatible long-term goals on major issues, such as career goals and where to live? Are you reasonably confident you can achieve these goals together?

13. Is he supportive emotionally and spiritually?

14. Will you be able to count on him in a time of personal crisis (illness, bereavement, job loss, financial despair)?

15. If you were ill or dying, would you entrust him to make medical decisions on your behalf and care for your children?

16. Does he give comparably or more than he takes from the relationship?

17. Can he get over his anger, frustration, or disappointment in a constructive way?

18. Is he polite, not just with you, but also with friends, family, colleagues, and strangers?

19. Does he take care of himself and encourage you to do the same? Is he a positive and healthy influence?

20. Do you agree on whether or not to have children, and how many?

21. If you do desire kids, do you agree on major child-rearing issues, such as education, faith, health care, and discipline? (If neither one of you wants children, score four points for this question and skip to question 22.)

22. Do you accept each other's strengths and weaknesses, without trying to (dramatically) change each other?

23. Does he make your life easier, rather than creating more work or complicating matters for you?

24. Can you tolerate his personal commitments and burdens, including children from a past relationship, obligations to relatives, a physical disability, mental disorder, or addiction, or an all-consuming career, job, faith, or hobby?

25. Is he a good person, viewed by yourself and others as someone with strong moral convictions and high character?

FINAL SCORE:

90 – 100   **Grade:** A. Very good chance that you are with the right guy.

80 – 89   **Grade: B.** Good prospects, requires work to reach ideal category.

70 – 79   **Grade: C.** Further work required. He barely passed. Give serious thought about whether he's worth the time, effort, and risk.

Below 70   **Grades: D and F.** Move along! You are wasting valuable time.

What do you do if your man gets a low score, but you don't want to leave him? Some women whose mates score a C grade or below insist that love takes sacrifice and they are willing to tolerate shortcomings, even if they're significant. Many women fear that they won't meet anyone better, and are reluctant to hit the singles scene once again.

Let me tell you, even if you marry the most magnanimous Prince Charming on this planet, there will be sacrifices (just ask my wife). That's part of what marriage is about—promising to be with someone through good times and bad, agreements and disagreements. So the compromises and sacrifices you're making now are just the beginning, and will multiply if you plan to raise children together. It's important to set fairly high standards for a life partner, to avoid ending up miserable and resentful as you journey through the future together.

You should have aspirations for an A grade, but no worse than a B. If your candidate scores a D grade or below, your chances of happiness are being greatly compromised. I suggest ditching him. This isn't like taking a math course in college, where you could accept poor grades knowing you won't be using calculus after you receive your diploma. These are grades that you are signing up for personally over a lifetime, and any offspring must cope with the results as well.

If the guy scores a marginal grade of C, try to ascertain whether learning more about him can lead to a better score. Are there specific things that you or he can do to improve the relationship? For example, if his complaints about work are making your life together difficult, what happens if he finds a new job? Is he even willing to do so? Remember not to expect dramatic change. If he's always had a problem with overspending, your friendly budget advice probably isn't going to fix him.

Regardless of the scoring, plan on taking the test again in a month or two, especially if the relationship is new, or after passing a critical juncture (for example, after "the talk" on where your relationship is heading), to see if his score improves. If it doesn't, remember the reason why you took the test in the first place: You want to find out what kind of a long-term prospect this guy represents.

That's where my twenty profiles, detailed in the pages to follow, can help. In my research, I have found that relationship prospects tend to fit into certain patterns, with startlingly predictable sets of behaviors. Once you understand which profile(s) suits your guy, you'll gain valuable insight into the dynamics of your relationship. And you'll get handy tips to help you figure out whether there's hope for a lasting relationship with him—or if you should ditch him and put your energy toward finding someone better.

PART TWO

Twenty Profiles of Mr. Wrong

Profile I:
The Mystery Man

L ET ME TELL YOU ABOUT a lovely woman I know in Phoenix , Arizona . She had a wonderful time early in her courtship with a guy she dated for several years, sure that he was Mr. Right. He was handsome, charming, athletic, engaging, articulate, and polished. They had a great time on dates to eclectic restaurants, popular public events (courtside Phoenix Suns games, VIP tickets at the Phoenix Open PGA golf tournament, front-row seating at local concerts), and elaborate vacations to New York City, Las Vegas, Florida, and Mexico. She also enjoyed spending time with his many friends, who warmly received the couple at their affluent homes.

Then she started picking up signs of trouble. Special events and fancy dinners ceased. They only went on vacations she could pay for. "Prime-time" dates (Friday and Saturdays) evaporated. She suspected that he was cheating on her, as they didn't see each other as often, and he claimed to have more "business functions" in his schedule than normal. His interest in intimacy diminished. She also grew suspicious when she didn't see any returns from a business investment she made that he was overseeing.

Her family urged her to hire a private investigator, who uncovered some very alarming truths about her man. When they started dating, he had actually been engaged to another woman, with the wedding date only weeks away. He had three children out of wedlock with three different partners. His credit history was awful. There were even signs that he extorted money from elderly acquaintances and possibly his family. None of the friends she met were really close to him—they were basically part of extended social circles he'd claimed as his own. Even his college diploma was in question!

When she looked back on the years she wasted with this man, she realized she had ignored some very early warning signs that she filed away but failed to act on:

- His stories about where he was, what he was doing, and why he was getting late-night phone calls were vague and inconsistent.
- He overtly lied about or omitted important details of prior and present female relationships, and the children that he sired.
- She never fully comprehended how he made money.
- Close friendships were not apparent.
- After a certain point in their relationship, he was reluctant to pay for anything, even simple gifts when going to someone's home for a party.

Every man is a mystery at first. That's why you go on dates—to get to know one another better. Some men hold the cards closer to their chest than others. It may be their personal style, or they may enjoy sustaining your intrigue for a few weeks. They may be shy or have a private nature. Certain aspects of their personal life – a rough childhood, for example – may be difficult for them to discuss until they've built up trust with you. But no matter how smart, good-looking, or fun your man may be, you want to make sure that over time he becomes less mysterious, not more.

Follow your instincts. Is there a pattern of unusual or suspicious behavior? Do you feel like he's not just hard to get to know, but is actually hiding something? If you have a gut feeling that something is amiss, you should research the situation fully.

He may:
• Leave out pertinent details—especially ones that might make him look bad.
• Recite information as fact, only for you to learn that it is incorrect.
• Delay telling you crucial information about himself until you're emotionally attached.
• Outright lie to or deceive you.
• Be a compulsive liar, fabricating every detail of his life until you may not even be sure if his name is his own.

There are very few acceptable explanations for the above behavior. Some people are storytellers, given to embellishing the details to make their tales more dramatic or entertaining. This isn't necessarily a bad thing, but you should be able to have a good idea of what actually transpired and what he's making up for effect.

There's also the possibility that he forgets details or gets the facts wrong because he's not that bright. Then you have a whole other issue on your hands. Can you really get close to someone who's not your intellectual equal?

Timing is a delicate issue. When should a man tell a woman about his three divorces? His children from a past relationship? His drug trafficking conviction? Obviously he could be worried you'll judge him. But if he withholds crucial information after a dozen dates (three or four months into a relationship), you should be concerned. He is deceiving you by *omission*. Whether he means to or not, he's lured you into an emotional attachment that makes it more difficult for you to leave him, even if you're upset about what he's hidden from you. That's not fair.

Other signs your Mystery Man may be bad news:
• He has no close friends or longstanding relationships from different stages of his life (high school, college, places he's lived).
• Although some guys are bad at staying in touch, he may lack the depth of character to be a good friend.
• He isn't in touch with any family members or relatives.
• Be compassionate if he comes from a particularly troubled family, but you're entitled to learn why he's broken off contact.
• His friends seem shady.

• If you think his friends are creepy, find out why he's part of the crew.

• He's estranged from all of his former girlfriends.

• Everyone's had a relationship disaster or two, but if there are several shipwrecks in his love life, you need to investigate. You can learn a lot about people from the way they end relationships.

As you look into the life of your Mystery Man, *do there always seem to be more questions than answers?* If so, you may be in trouble.

If You're In Love with The Mystery Man:

There's hope if...

✳ He's private or shy by nature, yet every time you see him you feel you learn a little more about him.

✳ He has a very private profession that carries into his personal life (e.g., psychiatrist, law enforcement, attorney, private enterprise).

✳ He is in a high-pressure job and leaves his work at the office (e.g., oncologist, stockbroker, sales executive).

✳ He's had rough patches in his past, but he communicates openly and honestly and requests patience in return.

✳ He's cautious about opening up because he's been hurt in the past by friends, family, colleagues, or former significant others.

✳ His slight embellishments of the truth when he's telling a good story are fun and ultimately harmless.

Ditch him if...

✳ He lies so often you simply can't trust him.

✳ After six months of dating, you still don't feel you've gotten to know him any better.

✳ He seems completely alone in the world, with all of his past friendships, relationships, and family connections ending in conflicts he won't detail.

✳ You discover indications of a double life, such as another girlfriend, a hidden dubious profession, or unknown sources of income.

✳ He is a compulsive liar, with little truth to anything he says.

✳ He cannot, without hesitation, clearly detail what he does for a living and how he generates income.

Profile 2:
Mr. Rush Job

YOU CAN HARDLY BELIEVE YOUR good fortune. That hot guy you've been checking out—but hardly thought you had a chance with—actually noticed you. He's popular, often seen at the best nightclubs and parties, holding court with the ladies. He's also a bit cocky, but you view confidence as a plus. Much to your surprise, you've somehow captured his interest, and he invites you on a date. You're very flattered.

On the first date, he's flirtatious and showers you with attention. He's engaging and says all the right things. He's a perfect gentleman at dinner and doesn't overdo the wine. The date so far scores a perfect ten out of ten.

After dinner, he suggests continuing the evening at his place or boldly invites himself up to yours. You want to agree. You tell yourself you want nothing more than a first kiss, validating his interest in you and his desire to see you again.

But he's persistent. Once he does plant that first kiss on you, he gets more aggressive. Whether you are still in the car or in more private quarters, his hands are roaming and leaving little to the imagination. Although your body wants to keep going, your better judgment takes control. You push him back.

Once you separate, you tell him that you want to save something for another time. Suddenly, his demeanor changes. He becomes pushy, and possibly even borderline rude. He is clearly used to things going his way. You think of all the women who've probably given him exactly what he wants. What's wrong with giving in, anyway? You're wildly attracted to him, after all.

Do you:
    A. Sleep with him (You're a grownup, right?)?
    B. Put him off, at least until the second or third date?
    C. Abstain until you know him much better?
    D. Abstain until your wedding day?

Option D is realistic only for women with strong moral convictions about staying pure until marriage—and these women will probably seek out men who share these beliefs. If you're leaning toward option A or B, you're not alone. Plenty of men expect sex very early in a relationship. Plenty of women share that expectation, or decide to give in to please him.

My advice is: *Wait.* Choose Option C. Here's why.

You need to find out whether your new man is simply overeager or whether you've found yourself with Mr. Rush Job, the kind of man whose intent is to have sex with you as soon as possible, regardless of what follows. Mr. Rush Job may not care whether the sex leads to a relationship or not. He may even be averse to attachments that last beyond a night or two.

A friend I used to spend time with in my mid-twenties and early thirties was a real chick magnet. He was exceptionally smart and polished, seemingly a good catch, who made plenty of money and invested it judiciously. He'd start dating a woman and send every signal that the relationship was advancing in a positive direction. He wouldn't tell her outright that he wanted a future with her, but he would charm her to the point that she would infer this to be the case. But once he slept with her a time or two, he simply stopped calling. This happened time and time again. These jilted women would call him and pour their hearts out into the answering machine, while he sat idly by. They had no idea whether they'd done something wrong, or he was involved with someone else, or he'd lied about his feelings.

It got a little ridiculous. He never answered the phone himself—this was before caller ID. Whenever I called I'd have to let him know it was me and tell him to stop screening the calls and pick up. His pattern with women grew so extreme that he couldn't handle it when his friends got involved in healthy and enjoyable relationships.

What amazes me is that this guy could have had it all. Beautiful women would still flock to him, men would still idolize him, and he could feel good about his life. All he had to do was be honest about his wish to remain unattached. Instead, he cruelly misrepresented himself.

Try to get an honest answer from your pushy date that clarifies his intentions. Is he looking for little more than a physical relationship? A fun fling? These desires are quite normal. If he's honest with you from the outset, you shouldn't harbor hostilities when he moves on. If you wanted more, you should have made the decision to move on first. Not every guy you go out with is going to be a candidate for a husband. You are probably going to date lots of guys before finding Mr. Right. So even if the man you're with isn't The One, he'll be part of the learning experience that helps you develop your criteria for what you want or don't want in a partner.

Appreciate his candor, even if it means you learn something you don't want to know. A guy who tells it straight is a far better man than someone who feeds you lines and tells you he loves you by the third date. Don't fool yourself into thinking that your abilities in bed or overall charm will change his mind! They probably won't. If you still want to move forward with a physical encounter, go directly to The Hot Prospect Background Check, a quick guide to what you need to find out about a man before becoming sexually intimate with him.

What if your date fits that other possibility—he's simply overeager? He's interested in you as a potential girlfriend and wants to get close to you ASAP. Men will give in to their desires practically whenever the opportunity seems to present itself. In that case, you may ask, what's wrong with giving in?

Plenty. For many men, a woman who gets into bed with him too early is not a woman with long-term appeal. They may act frustrated or even rude if you refuse their advances, and if you give in, or initiate sex yourself, they'll be gratified for the moment. But they'll think about you later as too easy and not the girlfriend (or marrying) type. That sounds a little twisted, but it's true.

That's why women need to be the strong ones. They need to control when intimacy starts, without discouraging a good prospect. They need to do their due diligence to make an informed decision about whether starting a sexual relationship with a new man is a good idea.

If you find this burden chauvinistic or unfair, let me remind you of two biological realities:

1. Unintended pregnancy
2. Sexually transmitted disease (STD)

With an unintended pregnancy, you face the choice of having an abortion, if your value system permits it, or having the child, which could link you to Mr. Wrong for a lifetime (see "*What to Do If You Get Pregnant Unexpectedly*"). With an STD, you will deal with a condition that's uncomfortable for you and potentially a mark of damage in the eyes of future prospects.

Beyond these two big reasons not to have sex too soon, consider these possibilities:

You develop a reputation for having slept with a bad prospect (guilt by association).

He could become abusive, physically or verbally, during sex, endangering your safety and well-being.

You could find out he was a deadbeat dad, a criminal, or a similarly unsavory type, leaving you ashamed that you slept with him.

He could be mentally ill or a stalker, causing problems for you at work or home.

Spending time fooling around with Mr. Wrong could distract you from finding Mr. Right.

What sorts of questions are fair game before intimacy starts? Take a little time to get to know your prospective sexual partner. Observe his behavior and his social life. Get a sense of his past. One clue my ex-friend's conquests missed was that he had never been in a relationship that lasted longer than a few months and none of his friends seemed to have steady girlfriends. Intimacy issues, anyone?

The Hot Prospect Background Check, below, may seem alarmingly extensive. But I'm merely encouraging you to uncover the facts you'd potentially be horrified to find out about *after* sexual intimacy.

Exercise some discretion as you do your research, so he doesn't get insulted or judge you paranoid. No one likes to find out that a potential girlfriend has looked him up on the local sex-offender registry. But few will deny that it's important not to get involved with a rapist!

The Hot Prospect Background Check

✳ Make sure he isn't a convicted felon or sex offender by searching computerized databases or the local county courthouse.

✳ Make sure he is not married or in another (supposedly) committed relationship (see Profile 3: The Disengagement Partier).

✳ Gain some insight into past relationships:
- How long did they last?
- When did his last relationship end?
- Was the breakup amicable?
- Is he over the relationship?
- Do they remain in contact?

✳ Check references:
- Find someone credible who knows him fairly well and mention you've gone out with the man in question. Gauge the associate's reaction. Does he wince or make derogatory comments about The Hot Prospect's character or how he treats women?
- Learn what he does for a living. Is it something respectable, or something he feels he has to hide? (See "Ditch him if" advice in *Profile 1: The Mystery Man*.)

✳ Find out his basic religious beliefs and politics.
- Is he a member of a highly controversial religious sect or a political organization?

✳ Learn a little about his friends, family, and colleagues, spending time with them if possible.

- Is he involved in a gang?
- Are his friends or family serving time in prison or under investigation?
- Law enforcement officials frequently target girlfriends. If he is selling drugs or involved in other criminal activity, you could be seen as an associate.

It's not easy to wait, and the homework *The Hot Prospect Background Check* entails can be challenging. But waiting is worth it.

I have a good female friend in her late thirties who has been struggling on the dating circuit for years, trying to find Mr. Right. She met a man to whom she was very attracted. Soon after he started calling her, but before a first date, she decided to be spontaneous and accept his invitation to visit him late one night. He was so physically aggressive she became frightened; she realized she knew almost nothing about this guy and was completely vulnerable alone with him in his house. She wiggled her way out of trouble that evening. Later that week they talked, and he was extremely contentious. He made it clear she shouldn't come by again unless she expected to have sex with him.

The incident left a lasting psychological impact on her, making her leery of other men. If she'd taken the time to do The Hot Prospect Background Check, she very likely would have been able to screen this guy out as a presumptuous creep, or at least uncovered enough uncertainty to have proceeded with more caution. She would have gotten to know this guy better, and he would have quickly realized she wasn't going to be "easy."

If You're Entangled with Mr. Rush Job:

There's hope if...
* He understands that you need to get to know him better before you sleep together.
* You know him exceptionally well, have common acquaintances, and are comfortable with progressing to an intimate relationship.

✳ You do a thorough *Hot Prospect Background Check* and he comes up clean.

✳ You both want the same thing, whether it be casual fun or a potential long-term relationship.

✳ You have an escape plan and a reliable way to protect yourself against STDs and unintended pregnancy.

Ditch him if:

✳ The *Hot Prospect Background Check* turns up anything disturbing.

✳ You have different expectations for the relationship.

✳ He considers sex your obligation to him because he's spent money on you and treated you well.

✳ He is so sexually aggressive you feel intimidated or threatened.

✳ Your intuition leads you to believe that something just isn't right with the guy.

What to Do If You Get Pregnant Unexpectedly

You've recently started a sexual relationship with a new man, and you miss your period. You take a pregnancy test, twice to be sure. You're pregnant. What do you do?

✳ A big consideration is your age, and whether you intend to have children someday. This was probably not your dream scenario, but it's happened, and you need to evaluate whether you can make this work, with or without short- or long-term support from the sperm donor.

✳ Are you prepared to raise a child? It's an all-consuming, draining, yet satisfying experience. It's not for everyone. It is the ultimate selfless act. As you make your decision, you'll want to ask yourself:

• Do you know enough about the father to determine whether it's a good idea to propagate his genes with yours?

• Can you live with a long-term connection to this man?

• If well into your thirties, could this be a last chance to bear children?

• Can you raise a happy, healthy, and well-adjusted child?

✳ If your moral beliefs support it, abortion is an option. But even if you are sure you don't want to have a child, ending a pregnancy can be emotionally grueling. Talk to close friends, immediate family, and possibly your spiritual advisor. If you feel you need it, seek counseling. It's a huge decision, and something with which you will need to be at peace.

✳ Adoption is another alternative. Many childless couples wish to adopt domestically but are often pushed to adopting in China, South America, Africa, or Eastern Europe. Many women have mixed emotions once they go through a full term of pregnancy, though, and they often have a change of heart.

If you want to have the child:

✳ Be realistic. The father is not going to magically transform into Mr. Right because his sperm fertilized your egg.

✳ Take the Dating Litmus Test. If the guy scores a B or higher and wants to have a role in raising your child, then try to continue the relationship. Don't rush into marriage, though.

✳ If your man scores a C or lower, consult a lawyer, preferably before you tell your partner you're pregnant. Mothers typically get 20 percent of the father's gross income for child support. Don't believe the father's "I'll take care of you" rhetoric.

✳ Try to keep your relationship with the father friendly. It is in your best interest and in the best interest of your future child.

✳ If the father is a real loser who has little to offer financially or emotionally to you and your child, you may wish to go it alone if the father elects not to make any contributions, financially or emotionally.

Secondary issues if you consider bringing a baby into the world include:

✳ Career
- Can you take maternity leave?
- Will you still be able to carry out your job to full potential?
- Will having a child inhibit career growth and earning capability?

✳ Financial support
- Will the man provide child support?
- Does your health care plan or the father's cover childbirth and pediatric care?

✳ Child care
- Can you afford it?
- Will you have help from your family?

✳ Education
- Can you afford to pay for the child's education?

✳ Stigma of being a single mom (if you don't stay with the father)
- Some men may not be comfortable dating a woman with a child.

- Personal limitations
- The spontaneity in your life will be gone. No more last-minute happy hours, dates, dinner plans, movies, parties, or vacations.
- What will be your relationship with the father?

My primary advice as a married man to a single woman in this predicament is to act of your own volition. Don't lose your head; it's really not the end of the world. Take a few days or weeks to consider and weigh all of your options. It's great to get feedback from trusted sources, but you need to make a decision that you can live with. Do what is right for you, and potentially for the child you may bring into the world. This could be a temporary setback, or it could turn into one of the best experiences of your life!

Profile 3:
The Disengagement Partier

A FEMALE FRIEND FROM ILLINOIS SEEMS to readily find new boyfriends. She's soon infatuated and raves about them the first month. Then during the second month, she starts admitting the problems. One hot new man is still living with a prior flame (but of course they're not sleeping together). Another suitor reveals the divorce isn't final. She explains away the cordial relationship he maintains with his ex-wife as something he does "for the benefit of the children," but she has to stifle her anxiety when the almost-divorced pair seems to do a lot more together than a platonic relationship would entail.

After these romances go bust, she takes a while to admit the pattern: She's drawn to guys in transition. These men are merely testing the waters with a woman to whom they know they won't get attached, trying to decide whether they're really done with their present relationship or they want back in.

How much fun is it to date a guy for more than a couple of times, then find out the real reason that he hasn't invited you back to his place? How do you explain the fact that he's still married, or living with a supposed ex-girlfriend? Has the ex figured out that she's categorized as an ex, or is he really cheating on her with you?

What if he's finally left her, making you the primary girlfriend? Men are creatures of habit. Don't be surprised if he eventually has someone on the side, enjoying the perks of being the new girl. It's an easy rule of thumb: If a guy cheats and you are the object of his newfound affection, he may eventually turn the tables.

If he really has strong feelings for you, and has any class whatsoever, he'll sever the present relationship before engaging with you. This approach is the only respectful one for both women, and a positive reflection on him.

Before you insist that your man wipe his slate clean before spending time with you, a few words of caution. While you are casually dating, the "don't ask, don't tell" guideline is a fair policy. You don't really have the right yet to know how many women he has on speed dial. But if you've had the girlfriend/boyfriend talk and decided to be exclusive, then why should he retain his electronic black book? He should get rid of the numbers on his own. Otherwise, he's playing the odds that the relationship with you may not pan out, and he wants backup options readily available. He's keeping other candidates on ice as long as possible.

Understand that pictures and videos of his ex may take

longer to disappear. Don't be too surprised or jump to the wrong conclusions if you find pictures of old flames, even racy ones. Guys save such souvenirs to remind themselves of their younger, more decadent lives, trying to live vicariously through their fading memories. It's the same reason guys save the baseball cards and stamps they collected as boys. If you discover memorabilia you're uncomfortable with, try a little sarcasm-tinged humor, like, "I hope you weren't planning on placing that low-budget porn flick from your starving student days on YouTube?" or "Should I view the hard-body photos in your closet as a hint to buy that twenty-minute abs video?"

The Disengagement Partier may be more bitter than nostalgic, though. He may still be obsessing over the details of his breakup. Listen carefully, and try to be objective. If you find yourself sympathizing with his ex more than with him, be careful! How he handled the breakup can hold many clues about whether he is a strong candidate for a long-term relationship. If he was respectful and gentlemanly as the couple parted ways, he's worth a chance. If he constantly insults his ex-girlfriend with the "b" word, or worse, beware. His anger may be a way of life.

If he's overly jealous or possessive when his ex moves on to someone new, it is a sure sign of trouble. It's common for men to struggle when the mother of their children or former wife/girlfriend is getting intimate with someone else. But if he can't shake his envy, take it as a sign he's not completely over her yet.

Note: He may be justifiably concerned with who this new man is if his children are going to be spending time around him. These worries are *not* the same as sexual jealousy, especially if the ex's new guy does not appear to be a person of quality or high integrity. If his sole concern is directed at ensuring the welfare of his children, you must not intervene, and the situation may require patience and understanding.

At the very least, he may simply not be ready to move on. If that's the case, let him go. Getting a man on the rebound is a very risky proposition, and you can be hurt or waste valuable time and energy.

On the other hand, certain situations, such as with men in the process of divorce, do realistically require additional time. You may need to sit tight if he's a good prospect. He may be over the relationship and emotionally ready for someone new, but the marriage has not officially ended yet because he's posturing for his rightful share of the assets or dealing with tax consequences from the separation. His wife may be fighting the divorce proceedings or trying to reconcile. The situation can get enormously complicated if children are involved and he's fighting a custody battle in addition to scrambling for his share of material possessions and finances. The stakes are high.

Don't be selfless, though—if the stakes are too high and the battle is too heated, he may not be able to give enough attention to a new relationship, and his children may be a much higher priority than you at this point.

Speaking of children: It's important not to rush him into introducing you to his kids right away. They may be having a rough time accepting the divorce, or get confused by the introduction of a new partner for dad into the equation. Some men, on the other hand, may be too eager to get you into their children's lives.

Take the story of an Ohio woman who fell in love with an attractive and seemingly intelligent man who'd recently ended his longstanding relationship with the mother of his son; they'd had the son out of wedlock and amicably agreed upon joint custody. After just a few months of their romance, the new girlfriend was called upon to babysit the boy so her man could attend supposed business meetings. He was actually cheating on her with multiple partners while she worked for free as his nanny and house cleaner! How confusing this must have been for the boy, not to mention this woman, who was clearly hoodwinked!

In these scenarios, consider what you would want if the situation were reversed and you were the person with children from a former relationship. You would want to be darn sure that the relationship had substance and potential before introducing your children to a new guy, and that you had properly screened this new candidate (through the rigors of the Dating Litmus Test or otherwise). Your children may be even more vulnerable than you are.

If You Want a Lasting Relationship with The Disengagement Partier:

There's hope if...

✳ He has hope for the possibilities of a new and better relationship.

✳ After meeting you, he makes a clean break with his girlfriend (including moving out), then calls you up for a date.

✳ If married, he is open and honest about his divorce proceedings.

✳ He communicates cordially with his ex.

✳ If he has children, he discusses openly with you the question of when you should meet them.

Ditch him if...

✳ He's still living with someone else.

✳ He is obsessed with his ex, constantly complaining about her or compulsively calling her, as if to check up on her.

✳ There are any signs he's still involved with, attracted to, or sleeping with his ex.

✳ The more you learn about his breakup, the more you sympathize with his ex.

✳ The divorce is taking more than a year. The delay suggests some sort of problem or attachment that he cannot or does not wish to sever (divorce should be consummated within a year).

✳ He avoids introducing you to his children or persists in defining you as "just a friend" long after your relationship has progressed.

Profile 4:
The Student/Teacher

I**T'S WONDERFUL TO BE IN** a relationship where you can take turns learning something interesting, useful, or valuable from each other. You may possess an extensive knowledge of history or literature. He may be computer or Internet savvy. You may have a knack for decorating, while he may encourage you to share his zeal for mountain biking, hiking, or working out at the health club. You both may enjoy cooking and taking turns at being the chef du jour. He may have done exceptionally well in the stock market, while you've had a flair for investing in real estate.

You alternate being the teacher and the student. He's shared his passion for the opera, telling you all about his favorite composers and singers, and you're thrilled to finally have some insight into this new and fascinating world. Your routine has been watching the latest HBO series on Sunday nights and he now joins you, letting you get him up to date on the characters and plots. He loves sports, and you've found a way to share his fervor, as a participant or a spectator. Over time, you've turned Saturday poker nights with the boys into game night with mixed company. You both enjoy the sense of competition and camaraderie.

A man who shares his wealth of interests with you and welcomes you to do the same may indeed be a keeper. It's entertaining, inspiring, and beneficial to learn so much.

You may find that one member of the couple takes on the teacher role more often, making most of the decisions and social plans. That's fine, but don't always let him take the lead! Even if your man seems naturally more assertive than you are, he needs to share his power.

If he doesn't, he may really be more a taskmaster than a teacher. He may dominate too much, or become overly controlling (see *Profile 8, The Man in Control*). As the student, in turn, you may become insecure or lose self-esteem. After the initial thrill is gone, you may resent always being seen as inferior, and he may resent you for not being smarter or more sophisticated.

You also need to ask yourself, is all this teaching and learning merely a cover-up for the fact that you have very little in common with your man? If you genuinely enjoy what he's into, and he unabashedly embraces your hobbies, that's great. But sometimes the initial turn-on of having your new man help you into a yoga pose can distract you from the fact that you really don't like yoga much. You'll soon tire of pretzel twists and back bends, and you'll find something else to do while he's standing on his head.

Giving each other space to go in different directions is certainly healthy. It's okay if you don't develop a long-term interest in everything he introduces you to and vice versa. Sometimes it's actually nice to do things on your own or with other people.

But as you get to know each other, you need to ask yourself whether you really have enough in common. I've heard of couples going on vacations and spending all their time—except meals and sleeping together—on mutually exclusive activities. I'm not talking about the one day the gal goes to the spa and the guy plays golf. I'm talking about the *entire* vacation. If that's the case in your relationship, you may want to ask yourself whether this is really what you had in mind for a permanent partnership.

Years ago in Silicon Valley, a lady friend who had a steady boyfriend invited me, Mr. Corporate, to be her date for every social event at her company. I would mix and mingle, entertaining her friends and engaging in business talk with her colleagues. She shared her personal life with her significant other but needed an entirely different support group for her professional life. He had no interest in sharing corporate life with her. She knew that he wouldn't fit in. Needless to say, the relationship didn't last.

Sometimes a well-educated woman falls for the local hero, the handsome jock, or simply one of the more popular and debonair guys around town. She drags him along to concerts and plays. He loves it when she sits in the cheering section for the local baseball team he pitches for. Gradually, it dawns on her that he doesn't have much to say after they leave the theater, and she's truly bored by the baseball games. She starts to worry that this prospect lacks depth of both intellect and character, especially since she's grown emotionally attached to him. What to do now?

You may really enjoy the first months with a man who's very different from you, but do you really want to spend the rest of your life with him? If you love to read, can you handle his lack of interest in books? How will you feel if you cook an elaborate gourmet dinner for two and he turns it down in favor of a snack from the local fast-food eatery? Will you be disappointed hiking to the top of a beautiful mountain alone because he hates to exert himself? What will you do if you can barely agree on what to watch on television, or which movie to see?

Do you find yourself getting bored? Are you making a mental laundry list of idiosyncrasies that will simply grow intolerable?

Often, women in a fading student/teacher relationship hang on to the one or two things they do have in common with their man, or the one goal they share. This single point of connection may become the sole reason the relationship endures, despite hundreeds of signs that it shouldn't.

A couple from the Southeast met when she was in her mid-thirties and he was in his early forties. They had one thing in common: They wanted children. Beyond that, they didn't bother to diligently assess their compatibility. After dating a year, they got married. Differences quickly surfaced:

She was frugal, while he was carefree with his money, putting the relationship under enormous financial strain.

He enjoyed both participating in and watching sports, while she forbid him to turn on the game at home and never participated in anything remotely athletic.

She was sedentary and put on weight, while he was active and fit.

She had a taste for fine wine, and he drank beer and hard liquor.

He loved sushi and she couldn't stand the sight of raw fish.

She enjoyed reading and keeping up with current events, while he favored reality shows and read little more than the local newspaper's sports section.

She liked scheduling activities with her family, while he preferred his relatives.

She had her friends and he had his, and the two groups rarely mixed.

They had a baby together. They did share their love for the child they'd both wanted for so long, but that one point of connection wasn't enough. When he got home from work every day, she'd hand over the child and state that it was "his turn." Then she'd go off and do her own thing. The couple fought a lot and eventually sought marriage counseling. Therapy did little more than point out the extent of their incompatibility.

It's best to experiment with guys who are very different than you are early in your dating career. By the time you're well into your late twenties or early thirties, you really should be wiser. Pick someone who's a good match for you intellectually. Make sure you share more than sexual chemistry and curiosity. Don't fool yourself into thinking a man with whom you have little in common is magically going to take on all your interests and that you'll do the same with his. You don't want to be that classic scene of elderly ennui shown again and again on television shows and in the movies: the long-married old man and woman, all their children grown and gone, sitting at the dinner table together with nothing to talk about.

You don't want a future of perpetual boredom or, worse, disagreement when you pick a teacher whose lesson no longer appeals, or a student whose potential has disappointed. Do you really want to continue to pretend to enjoy the same old stories or corny jokes that have your eyes rolling? You want a partner who gets jazzed by many of the same things you do, and relishes the common ground you share, and continues to entertain and charm you.

If You're Sharing Your Life with Mr. Student/ Teacher:

There's hope if...

✳ You are sometimes the student, sometimes the teacher, sometimes equals, and you enjoy all these roles.

✳ You find your differences exciting and stimulating.

* You respect and admire each other's minds and are a good intellectual match.

* You have a lot in common to balance out your differences.

* You give each other space to enjoy activities or friends separately.

* You feel comfortable and at ease with him, even when he's the teacher.

Ditch him if...

* You feel stuck and resentful as the perpetual student.

* You feel impatient and bored as the perennial teacher.

* You realize that no matter how hard you've tried to find things to share, you really have very little in common.

* You find yourself thinking he's just not very smart or open-minded.

* You dread most one-on-one time with him (except for the physical connection).

* He confuses and intimidates you, diminishing your self-esteem.

Quiz: How Different Are You?

Complete each of the following statements by circling the answer that most closely fits. See below for scoring.

When I tell him about an upcoming social event with my circle of friends,

✳ he eagerly writes it on his calendar or makes a "mental note of it."

✳ he asks if he can invite a few of his friends as well.

✳ he gets jealous, intimates or hints at his disdain for the company I keep.

When he turns on the television,

✳ I sit down and watch with him.

✳ I join him sometimes, but it's no big deal if I don't.

✳ we argue, and rarely agree on what to watch.

After my partner and I go to the movies, we

✳ talk about the movie until late and then again in the morning.

✳ revisit parts of the movie from time to time.

✳ rarely have anything to say to each other about it.

My partner supports my career

✳ enthusiastically.

✳ sometimes, though his career clearly comes first.

✳ not much at all, because he doesn't really understand or care about what I do.

My partner's religion is
✳ the same as mine or comparable to what I practice.
✳ different, but neither of us is observant.
✳ different, and we have completely different approaches toward spirituality.

My partner likes to eat
✳ a similar diet to mine.
✳ a variety of foods, and we enjoy sharing new dishes.
✳ what I consider disgusting and inedible food.

When I read in bed, my partner
✳ grabs a book and settles in beside me.
✳ cruises the latest news on the Internet, sharing tidbits with me as he goes.
✳ is upset that I'm not paying enough attention to him.

When we wake up on a Saturday morning and the sun is shining, we're most likely to
✳ take a morning walk or plan something spontaneous outdoors.
✳ independently work out, but connect later to enjoy a pleasant day together.
✳ go our separate ways.

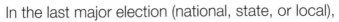

In the last major election (national, state, or local),

✳ we supported the same candidate.

✳ we respectfully agreed to disagree.

✳ we stopped talking about politics, since our opposing views are upsetting.

We both have vacation time coming up. We

✳ plan a week at a resort with some shared and several independent activities.

✳ coordinate an exotic, adventurous, and affordable vacation together.

✳ plan separate trips because the last time we vacationed together he was a drag, and we needed a break from each other.

SCORING

If most of your answers were "a," you are cozy compatibles. You have plenty in common.

If most of your answers were "b," you are spontaneous sweeties. Your energy and spirit of adventure make mild differences seem insignificant.

If most of your answers were "c," you are deleteriously different. Are you with the right person? Retake the *Dating Litmus Test* to see if your score is taking a nosedive.

Profile 5:
The Benefactor

A WOMAN FROM SOUTHERN CALIFORNIA MET a terrific guy. He came from an affluent family and managed both his business interests and inherited wealth judiciously. After a short courtship, he encouraged her to move into his palatial home. Her relocation package included room and board, a car, and frequent vacations. She didn't have to shell out a dime for any of it, so she stopped working. She assumed that he wouldn't have bestowed all these riches on her if he wasn't serious about her.

After a few years, he became bored. His physical attraction to her waned, and he broke up with her. She had to try to resurrect a career with two empty years as stay-at-home girlfriend on her résumé. Needless to say, she also had to revise her budget, as he'd stopped paying for everything.

Meet The Benefactor. At first, he wines and dines you in high style. Then he takes you to exotic and enjoyable retreats, where you're pampered in the luxurious surroundings of the Bellagio in Las Vegas or the Four Seasons Resort at Mandalay Bay. You accompany him on business trips to the Bahamas, Baja California, or Hawaii. During the day, you bask in the sun, reading a romance novel. At night, you sip mai tais together, watching the sun set. Some of these trips are spontaneous, and you try not to think about how your boss was upset that you couldn't give him more notice before you took those extra few days off.

In fact, you try not to think about work at all. You're not needing the money as much these days. He can easily take care of expenses that were a stretch for you before: rent, groceries, utilities, entertainment and recreation, health care, clothing, car payments, personal grooming, whatever arises. He might even cover your credit card debt.

Congratulations, you've just received the *dating scholarship*. If you haven't met this guy, you may be saying to yourself, "Where do I sign up?"

The benefits can be incredible. It feels great to enjoy a level of comfort, emotionally, financially, and professionally, that you didn't envision having so quickly. Maybe you've elevated your standard of living, or you've started to save more of your income.

But beware: When the honeymoon period is over, The Benefactor may need to tackle increasing responsibilities at work, spending more time in the office or traveling. You'll grab at any time you can get with him, even if it means canceling other commitments at the last minute. At first you'll have no problem accommodating him, since you welcome the chance to be together.

You may not make a big deal of it early in the relationship, but you notice that he still finds time to play golf on the weekends. He accepts every dinner invitation from customers or co-workers, no matter how impromptu. You are invited along less often. He spends his lunch hour at the gym instead of stealing away for a meal with you.

Time progresses and you start to quiz him about why you don't spend more quality time together. He quips that he returned home early a few times recently but you weren't home yourself, as if suggesting that you should be at his beck and call. When you do find a moment together, he's tired and stressed, or his mind is wandering elsewhere.

If you were financially challenged and have come to enjoy the improved standard of living, you tolerate most of this behavior and continue to oblige. You may find that this guy becomes controlling, requiring you to limit your work or personal activities to accommodate his unpredictable schedule. I've actually heard of men offering financial incentives to women to keep them at home.

What you may not realize is that you may be losing your sense of identity, purpose, control, and independence.

It's a completely different scenario if you get married, have children, and agree on the roles that each of you will play within the home. If the collective decision is that he works and you stay at home to care for the kids, so be it. You're agreeing to take on the worthy and valuable (and difficult!) job of raising children while he keeps the family afloat financially.

But when women become dependent on a man before they're truly committed to each other, they take a huge risk. Without money or a job of their own, they could lose ground financially and professionally. I'm not telling you that if you meet a great catch with the means to support you, you should be eternally pessimistic, but you also shouldn't defer personal ambitions and plan because someone else is looking after you, especially not before you're married or otherwise firmly committed. Nor should you lose your identity. You should maintain some of your individual passions and life objectives. If you make yourself happy, you're more likely to be able to make someone else happy. If the relationship sours, you'll have the sense of self to go back out on your own.

If You Find Yourself in the Moneyed Embrace of The Benefactor:

There's hope if ...

✳ You stay committed to your professional and personal life.

✳ You don't let yourself rely completely on him, emotionally or financially.

✳ You save money in case you need to go back out on your own.

✳ You use the dating scholarship to pursue a different career path, develop new skills, or advance your education.

✳ You recognize that your new lifestyle is not worth losing your self-esteem, identity, and independence.

Ditch him if...

✳ He's pressuring you to neglect your career, friends, and family to be available at his whim.

✳ He makes you feel your time is less valuable than his.

✳ He puts unreasonable conditions (such as leaving your job or ending a friendship) on the dating scholarship.

✳ Work always takes priority over time with you.

✳ You are in love with the financial security he provides, not him!

Profile 6:
The Underachiever

●●●◐◐●●◐●◐●◐●◐●◐●◐●◐●◐●●◐●

A WOMAN FROM MAINE WAS SUCCESSFUL in business, earning a good amount of money but contributing most of her savings to her needy extended family. She met a struggling yet charming construction worker who wanted to design homes, his true passion. On their third date, she discovered that he was married but wasn't in love with his wife. He eventually divorced the wife and moved in with her.

He encouraged her to find a better job to earn more money, while doing nothing to improve his own career. He saw himself as a misunderstood artist; his house designs didn't get the recognition they deserved because they were too sophisticated for prospective buyers to appreciate. He didn't want anyone to control him or how he did his work, and he grew increasingly frustrated. Much to her dismay, he started drinking and smoking dope. When he also became abusive, she sought counseling. She came to realize that it was important to her to be with a man who had a steady income and was not dependent on her. She ended the relationship.

The Underachiever may be a man of advanced intellect, natural talent, valuable experience, and great charisma, but for some reason, he can't or won't leverage any of these advantages in order to achieve. The causes can vary widely. He could lack discipline or drive. Maybe he never discovered what he truly wanted to do in life. Or perhaps his passion was impractical (making it as a rock musician or a professional athlete, for example) but he never gave up the dream, working odd jobs he didn't care about just to make ends meet. He could tend toward bad decisions or struggle with authority. He could also be caught up in vices, such as gambling, binge drinking, or recreational drug use.

Underachievers may seem like obvious bad catches. They aren't successful, or they haven't decided what they really want to do with their life. They don't have much money as a result. If they have it, it's inherited, and they may fritter it away irresponsibly or use it to fund their complacent or decadent lifestyle.

But Underachievers do have a certain appeal. They may seem too free-spirited or individualistic to "play the game" of advancing at work—or to hold down a job at all. They may be dashing, rebellious, and creative. If they lack self-confidence, the tender caretaker in you may be moved to help. Every Underachiever has one thing in common: tremendous *potential.* Could you be the inspiration that finally helps him accomplish his goals?

Sadly, you probably can't. If he's quite young, he may find himself and get on the right track. But if he's in his mid-thirties or older, it will be extremely challenging for him to reverse years of downward mobility. It's even more challenging for you to try to make him do it, even if your heart breaks over all his untapped potential.

So it's crucial to evaluate your man based on how he is now, rather than how you imagine he'll be if you change him. If you're with an underachiever and you haven't taken the Dating Litmus Test yet, be sure to do so ASAP. You may find that you've been so distracted by trying to make him Mr. Right or pitying him that very few of your own needs are being met.

You may, in fact, be entangled with a man who can't get along with others or can't follow a schedule. You may be falling for a guy who is too insecure to make the most of his natural talents. As charming as he is, he may also be bitter and unhappy. He may not even want to work hard to please you. After all, he's used to underperforming.

The Underachiever may have no savings, no retirement plan, and no health insurance. He may not be able to afford to go on vacation. All this may be his business now, but it becomes your business as well if you get married.

Life with an Underachiever takes a lot of acceptance, both on his part and yours. You may find yourself mired in struggle, as one woman from New York did when her husband's change in career path meant taking a more than 50 percent cut in compensation and led to even less career satisfaction. Or you may relish The Underachiever's lack of dependence on career success to feed his ego. A Boston man finally found his passion after several job changes, though he wasn't earning as much as he had earlier in his career. He and his wife happily started a family. His inner peace makes him a wonderful and caring father and a dependable husband.

Some Underachievers reject killer ambition in favor of spending more time on family or personal life. There may be compromises. You may not head for the French Riviera on vacation, or have a second home in Florida or a time share in Aspen. Your children may be headed to public schools and state colleges instead of private institutions. These concessions can all be fine if they feel like his (and your) choice, and the decision is largely based on establishing a *life balance.*

Be honest with yourself about what you can and cannot accept. If you are planning on having children, will you be able to afford the lifestyle and education you'd like them to have, or can you tolerate less? Will you be able to cope with the prospect of going back to work when your kids are small, without resenting your partner for failing to make enough money for you to afford to be a stay-at-home mom? Can you manage knowing that you may not retire as early as hoped?

It's important to distinguish between the need men may have to "find themselves" at a certain life juncture and the plight of The Underachiever. If your man has always been steady and dedicated but has hit a professional or personal wall, that's very different from a man in his late thirties or older who's never found his calling. The first guy needs to get over a hump, the second over a mountain! So if your man is going through a rough spot, be patient and give him enough space to find his way. If he remains unhappy, it will be very challenging for him to make his woman or potential children happy.

If You're Ambitious About Your Relationship with The Underachiever:

There's hope if...

※ He is basically at peace with himself.

※ He is secure enough to support your endeavors and accomplishments.

※ He manages, even with his limited career, to save and plan for the future.

※ He is reliable and trustworthy, even if he's not very ambitious.

※ You can honestly accept him for who he is, not for his "potential."

※ You can give him space for his creative endeavors, even if he doesn't earn significant income.

Ditch him if...

※ He is an utterly unhappy person.

※ His failures make him constantly frustrated and anxious.

※ His low self-confidence causes him to resent you and your abilities.

※ He frequently vents anger and jealousy about the successes of others.

※ He constantly blames others for his failures.

※ You can't imagine life with someone who is less successful than you are and who may depend on you financially.

Profile 7:
The Debate Champion

●●●●●●●●●●●●●●●●●●●●●●●●

M ANY COUPLES ARGUE. THEY ARGUE about chores, financial pressures, what to eat, or where to go. They argue about who forgot to do what, who didn't listen well enough, or who didn't dress properly for the last office party. They argue about friends or family, what to watch on television, weight gain, and other aspects of appearance.

Arguing may be their communication style. They may find arguing a form of intellectual stimulation, friendly competition, or even foreplay.

But some combative types have more malicious motives. Their confrontational style is about control, competition, hostility, or even hatred.

If you're with a man who argues, how do you know what's behind it? Is he crossing a line, or should you just accept his tirades as part of his demeanor—or your style as a couple?

Try to take an outsider's perspective. I know couples that argue relentlessly and publicly, disrespecting each other overtly, airing their conflicts to the point of making others uncomfortable in their presence.

My wife and I went out with a couple and had to listen to the woman openly ridiculing her husband on his bedroom manner. She shared intimate details that were offensive and embarrassing.

Another friend ridiculed his girlfriend's body openly, not at all sensitized to the fact that she had raised three children and Mother Nature had taken her toll.

These Debate Champions were treating their partners with disrespect and made their friends witness their bad behavior. These types of relationships are often unhappy. A woman I interviewed called them *toxic couples* and recommends avoiding them altogether. They can have a detrimental impact on your own relationship. You're exposed to behavior that should not be tolerated, including insults, condescending remarks, and other kinds of verbal abuse potentially damaging to self-esteem. If you take sides with one partner, you could end up alienating your own partner if he's loyal to the other.

Are you in a couple that others would consider toxic? Is your Debate Champion using tactics such as insults and forms of intimidation that make your friends cringe? It's easy to become myopic about your own romance and rationalize your partner's bad behavior. Your friends can more readily spot the deep-seated hostility in what you may interpret as excusable lapses. So if they are warning you about your man's behavior, listen. True friends usually are more than eager to cheerlead the new romances of their single friends. So if they aren't doing so this time, pay attention and don't get defensive.

You may also be blinded by post-reconciliation passion and the great make-up sex that can follow arguments.

An old roommate of mine fought constantly with his longtime girlfriend. The conflicts were abusive and public, worsening over time. What kept them together was the romance that followed their disputes. To their circle of friends, the two mixed like oil and water, but my roommate and his girlfriend were adamant about how "compatible" they were. In the end, he went over the line, going off to Hawaii to visit another woman under the guise of visiting an ailing grandmother in the Midwest. Because all their arguments had eroded her trust, she checked out his story with a travel agent friend, who couldn't locate his booking to mid-America. She did find a flight itinerary to Honolulu, though, and later review of his monthly phone bill revealed more than forty calls to Hawaii.

A guy with an argumentative nature doesn't necessarily spell disaster. You may not always be The Opposition. In fact, The Debate Champion can be your fiercest advocate, helping you develop a strategy to confront an oppressive boss or co-worker. Debate Champions will take on the maître d' if you have to wait too long for a table at a restaurant, or confront a good friend who's making bad choices. As fathers, they'll stand up at a school board meeting to argue against a new policy that isn't in their child's best interest.

But if you are someone who cringes at the first sign of an argument, don't fool yourself. If heated disagreements cause you to shut down emotionally, causing unnecessary stress levels, you may need to locate a significant other who is sensitive to your psychological makeup. The Debate Champion may not be a good match for you.

It is important to keep in mind that some amount of conflict is healthy. Couples sometimes avoid arguing so vigilantly during courtship that they fail to learn how to work amicably through natural conflicts.

One couple I know met in their late thirties. Both were people who wanted very much to find a spouse and had been searching for the right match for years. While dating, they never even so much as disagreed over anything. They married six months after they met. But as soon as she moved in—you guessed it!—the arguments started. She didn't approve of anything he did without her—exercising, playing golf, hanging out with single friends, taking business trips—even though he'd done these activities with impunity while they were dating. The marriage failed. She couldn't accept him for who he was, trying instead to convert him to her idea of a proper husband. More important, they never learned to communicate disagreements during their honeymoon period, so once conflict started, they didn't know how to handle them. See "Conflict Resolution Tips for Couples," below, on the fine art of working it out.

If You're Deliberating Life with The Debate Champion:

There's hope if...

✳ You truly enjoy debating.

✳ You are respectful and productive when you need to work out differences.

✳ You can disagree without being disagreeable.

✳ You and your partner know how to give each other space (e.g., avoid fights) when one of you is going through a difficult time, personally, physically, or professionally.

✳ You come out of the disagreement feeling good about the progress that you and your partner made, without having to compromise your beliefs.

✳ You can accept the times when you simply can't agree, and move forward.

Ditch him if...

✳ You can't stand arguments and need someone with a softer style.

✳ He persists in making condescending or insulting remarks about you in public, even after you've asked him to stop.

✳ He's a compulsive "devil's advocate," sparring and disagreeing with you on every subject and putting you down at every opportunity.

✳ Your reconciliations are the only times you feel a real

connection, sexual and otherwise.

✳ Your self-confidence has taken a nosedive from all the fighting.

✳ You feel like you're always making compromises, and your health or self-esteem is suffering as a result.

Conflict Resolution Tips for Couples

✳ If your significant other does or says something upsetting, don't take immediate offense. Ignore the topic briefly, about fifteen to twenty minutes, longer if necessary. Do something else to distract yourself. Work, read, exercise, watch TV, or listen to music. If the issue still bothers you, talk to your partner. Most of the time, what ticked you off becomes a non-issue after you've taken a break.

✳ Eliminate distractions when talking about conflicts. Turn off the TV or music and don't accept calls. Avoid bringing up problems late at night, as his attention span may be dead for the evening. Take it from my wife: The few times she's chosen to broach difficult subjects at night, it's been a disaster. I can sleep through a hurricane, and she lies in bed with her eyes wide open all night, waiting for me to wake up and resume the dialogue.

✳ *Men Are from Mars, Women Are from Venus* said it first: Men want a quick fix, while women sometimes just want to be heard. Remind him about what you need with the following preface: "I know it may be tough for you, but I want you just to listen. Don't try to fix anything, just hear what I have to say. I'll feel much better afterwards."

✳ Timing is crucial. If you or your significant other is

dealing with disappointments at work, or hosting a dreaded family member from out of town, or under an exceptional amount of stress, it's probably not a suitable time to bust his chops about his poor communication skills. Wait until equilibrium returns or the dust settles.

✳ Allow each other space before and after work. Don't expect him (or yourself) to rush back from work to sort out a conflict that began that morning. Take some time to unwind and relax before you resume the discussion. If you return home hungry, eat first. Low blood sugar is bad for conflict resolution.

✳ Conflicts should be raised and resolved in private, within the confines of your home. If they get aired in public, you risk embarrassing your partner or being humiliated yourself.

Profile 8:
The Man in Control

A MAN WHO TAKES CHARGE CAN be very alluring. He knows the right place to go for dinner and takes the check every time. He buys you clothes he's sure will look good on you, and glows with pleasure when you model the new outfits. He knows where he's going in life. He is confident and authoritative in leadership positions. He's an alpha male, and there's not a passive bone in his body.

You're glad to be with a *real* man, someone who knows who he is and how to get what he wants. You let him sweep you off your feet, surrendering to his judgment. He seems to know better than you, and you appreciate the guidance.

The Man in Control might have first discovered his true nature as the class brain in elementary school, as a sports star during adolescence, or as the student body president in college. He then cultivated his drive to lead in the workplace, using his talents with Darwinian "survival of the fittest" ambition to get to the top. He has also tended to be the one in charge in his circle of friends and extended family.

The Man in Control offers the material benefits of his

success and the attention his underlings, eager to please him, will bestow on you as the boss's girl. The Man in Control can be sophisticated, successful, confident, magnanimous, and sexy. He has the ability to make a positive difference at work, in his family, and in the world.

A lot of power professions—lawyer, police officer, corporate executive—require the ability to give orders to subordinates, clients, or the public. My wife knows this type first hand. After more than fifteen years as an executive, I was used to barking out orders to anyone who would listen. Though I never boss my wife around, she does permit me to take my managerial role home with me in many ways. She expects me to take the lead in many significant family decisions, such as major purchases, where to go on vacation, and what goes in our investment portfolio.

She doesn't mind at all, and in fact enjoys having me take charge. It's less pressure for her. In other areas—child rearing, health care, business accounting, home decorating, and other creative endeavors—she's the boss, or we're equal partners. Anytime there's confusion, a good talk quickly clears things up.

The Man in Control may be a strong candidate for Mr. Right, especially for women who prefer to let their partner be in charge. Even so, you'll want to make sure The Man in Control thoroughly understands your desires and expectations for the future. If you think you may want to keep working after having children, let him know so he doesn't expect a stay-at-home mother for his children. You'll need to find out whether The Man in Control can handle sharing childcare responsibilities and being in a dual-career couple.

If The Man in Control never seems to be able to turn off the boss attitude, you should ask yourself: Is your man in control, or *controlling?* A controlling man seeks out weaker people to dominate in order to empower himself and feel more secure. He looks for a significant other who will depend on him utterly, who is willing to follow, who will overlook his deficiencies, and who will *always* let him decide.

Take the story of a young California hair stylist who married a classic Man in Control. He was ten years older than she was, and far along in a lucrative career. She loved the nice home, the extravagant dinners, the financial support, and the lack of worry over major decisions. But there were problems. She liked to go out to happy hours after work a few times a week with her young friends. She didn't stop after he told her he disapproved—she just started sneaking out. He pushed her to get a breast augmentation, even though she didn't want it and many of her friends felt she didn't need it. He checked up on her to see if she was telling the truth about where she was and whom she was with. She ventured farther from his grasp when he was busy at work, and she eventually uncovered an entirely different life that was far more gratifying than the stifling existence she shared with him. She met other men who made her feel special, not captive. The couple divorced shortly thereafter.

A controlling man is not confident, at least not inside. He is deeply insecure, and quite possibly inept and inadequate. He may not be able to hold down a job, stay physically healthy, or truly love another person—which, as we all know, requires letting go of control sometimes. He masks these faults by manipulating others to do his will.

He can't take no for an answer, and won't tolerate disagreement or dissent. He'll want to know your every move, and he'll make it abundantly clear if he doesn't like where you're going or the people with whom you're spending time. He may not trust you to be outside the house on your own. Even if you give him no reason to be suspicious, he'll be thinking of how *he* feels when he's on his own, tempted to check out other prospects.

A controlling man's tactics might seem generous, à la The Man in Control, but there's usually a dark twist. Beware of the man who offers to let you live with him, rent-free, under the condition that he must have veto power over your social plans. Watch out for the man who insists that you get plastic surgery, or even a tattoo (with his name on it, of course) that you're not comfortable with. He wants to leave his mark on you, literally, sealing your surely troubled future together.

If you think you're with a controlling man, watch out. His tactics can become abusive, if they haven't already. You should not delay ending a relationship with a man exhibiting the "ditch him if" characteristics below. Go directly to

"Getting Rid of Mr. Wrong in Ten Easy Steps" in Part Three. You might need counseling and introspection to understand why you were attracted to this man in the first place.

If You're Under the Sway of The Man in Control:

There's hope if...

✷ He respects you to make your own personal decisions.

✷ You can communicate about disagreements in a productive way (see Profile 7: The Debate Champion for more details).

✷ He accepts and appreciates your friendships and obligations outside the relationship.

✷ Though at first he may take the lead on where to go and what to do on dates, eventually there's a healthy give and take.

✷ You feel confident sharing your opinions and thoughts with him.

✷ He supports your pursuit of what makes you whole or happy.

Ditch him if...

✷ He intimidates you.

✷ He judges your appearance, insulting you if you don't dress or look exactly as he wishes.

✷ He dominates your social schedule, becoming jealous when you attend business or personal events without him.

✷ He is always trying to convince you to agree with him, shooting down your individuality.

✳ He tries to limit (or end) your career so you can focus on his needs.

✳ He pressures you to do what he wants in the bedroom, ignoring your desires and making you feel uncomfortable (see *Profile 19: Mr. Twisted, Sister*).

Are You in an Abusive Relationship?

Domestic violence, also referred as domestic abuse, occurs all too frequently in intimate relationships. Domestic abuse can be verbal, emotional, physical, sexual, or a combination. The victims are mostly women, with approximately four million per year alone affected in the United States.

You may be involved with an abuser if your man:

✳ Berates, insults, or intimidates you

✳ Insists on isolating you from friends and family

✳ Strongly discourages you from going to work, school, or social events

✳ Dominates almost every aspect of your life

✳ Controls finances so you have to ask for money

✳ Is jealous or possessive, or accuses you of being unfaithful

✳ Forces you to have intercourse or to accommodate detested sexual demands

✳ Has fits of rage or destroys personal property

✳ Drinks excessively or is involved in substance abuse

✳ Threatens harm to himself or drives recklessly

✳ Grabs you hard, yells at you, or scolds you

✳ Looks at you or acts in ways that scare you

✳ Physically harms or threatens you, your children, or your pets

✳ Blames you for his violent behavior or tells you that you deserve it

✳ Demands abusive behavior is no big deal or even denies doing it

✳ Appears to be a completely different person than you've known

✳ Prevents you from calling the police or seeking medical care

✳ Appeals to you to drop potential charges

After such behavior, he apologizes profusely and promises he'll never repeat what he's done. The apology may be heartfelt, and you are convinced that this incident is an aberration. After you make up, you may experience a time of exceptional closeness.

You give him a second chance. You don't want to be alone—and there have been so many good times! You believe that leaving makes you a failure. You're ashamed to admit you chose a man who treated you this way. You convince yourself you may have overreacted or even imagined the incident, unless you have any physical marks that remind you.

But no rationalization will erase this simple fact: If you've experienced any of the above from your man, you have met the ultimate Mr. Wrong, The Abuser.

No matter how sweet the make-up, it won't last. In fact, it's an integral part of the Cycle of Violence, first described by Leonore Walker in her 1979 book *The Battered Woman:*

Stage One: Tension Building —You're walking on eggshells, careful not to upset him.
Stage Two: Explosion—Abuse occurs.
Stage Three: Honeymoon—There's apology and intimacy.
Stage Four: Denial—As long as denial exists for either partner, the abuse will continue.

You should end this relationship. Leaving may be difficult or, if you're with a physically violent man, even dangerous. Seek counseling. If you don't know where to start to find help in your community, contact The National Domestic Violence Hotline at 1-800-799-SAFE (7233). Other excellent resources for information are The National Coalition Against Domestic Violence website (http://www.ndvh. org) and the Mayo Clinic website (http://www.mayoclinic. com/health/domestic-violence/WO00044).

Abusive relationships are about power and control. Although there are no typical victims of domestic violence, abusive relationships do share similar characteristics. In all cases, the abuser aims to exert power and control over a partner. Many who are misinformed think domestic violence is about anger. It really isn't. Though batterers do tend to take their anger out on their intimate partner, their actions are ultimately about trying to instill fear and wanting to have power and control in the relationship.

Advice:

If both partners engage in verbal or psychological abuse, without a physical element, counseling may be helpful.

If you grew up in an abusive household, you may require some professional counseling before you can maintain a healthy relationship.

If your partner threatens physical abuse or you suspect he may become violent, you should sever the relationship.

Even one act of physical abuse means the relationship should be ended immediately to break the cycle.

If you have young children, contact school administrators and review custody arrangements. Take legal and logistical precautions, especially if your partner is the father or a legal guardian.

If you don't have a safe or affordable place to go, contact a women's shelter.

If your partner harms you or is in a regular pattern of abusive behavior, seek assistance immediately through law enforcement and/or counseling to protect yourself and take the necessary steps to end the relationship.

Profile 9:
Mr. Triathlete

MONTHS—OR EVEN YEARS—AGO, YOU MET a great guy. Part of his appeal was that he enjoyed staying in shape and worked out regularly. Your weekends together often included running, biking, skiing, tennis, golf, or a variety of other sports and outdoor activities. Vacations were planned to include physically challenging events, like hiking the highest peak in the Adirondacks or kayaking on the Columbia River. You enjoyed the endorphin rush of exercising together, and that feeling of well-being contributed greatly to your emotional and sexual connection.

But as your relationship progressed, he grew less interested in staying active. Perhaps increased work demands have left him too busy and worn out to do much more than sack out on the couch after work with a bowl of chips and a beer in front of him. Perhaps moving in together has decreased his motivation to plan special outings together. Or he has just gotten complacent or too comfortable to push himself to stay in shape. Another possibility is that he has just become downright lazy!

You worry that you seem to have less in common these days. He's also starting to gain weight, and you are finding him less sexually attractive as a result. It used to be foreplay when he walked around the house shirtless or came out of the shower, but now it's a turn-off.

You find yourself joking that your guy has turned into a "real triathlete," and we you don't mean the traditional iron man who can compete in a rigorous course of running, swimming, and biking. Mr. Triathlete walks from the couch to the refrigerator. Then he clicks the remote. Then he hops into the car and heads for the fast-food drive-thru.

You don't want to nag. You ask yourself, "What's wrong with putting on a few pounds?" But you can't ignore the fact that Mr. Triathlete isn't the quite the same man you fell in love with.

Your concerns are significant. Two-thirds of Americans are classified as overweight, meaning fifteen or more pounds over the healthy weight range for their age, height, and sex. If your man is falling prey to this national epidemic, there are plenty of reasons to worry. His health may be at stake, as overweight people are at greater risk for diabetes, heart disease, arthritis, and other endemic problems.

If you were to marry and reproduce with The Triathlete, his condition might even affect the health of your future children. Researchers at the University of Michigan found that if one parent is obese or overweight, their teen has an 80 percent chance of being overweight, probably because of a combination of genetics and family behavior (your husband could be a poor role model).

And then there is the question of your guy's mental health. Whether or not he wants to admit it, he's probably missing those endorphins. His weight gain may be contributing to depression. Or if he was already depressed, that's why he stopped working out. If he's having trouble being happy with himself, he's probably not making you very happy.

Speaking of which, your man may even be letting himself go because he's dissatisfied with your relationship. It's not the best way to cope with the problem, to be sure, especially if he wants out and plans to get back in the dating scene. But some men just can't handle settling down, and they take their disappointment out on their bodies.

An old friend was a real hunk of a guy in his youth, attracting women wherever he went. He had his pick of the hottest girls. After dating a woman for eight years, he finally got married. Then he started pigging out on junk food and stopped working out. He gained thirty pounds the year after the wedding. He wasn't motivated to keep his marriage in shape, either, and it didn't last.

So part of figuring out your man's weight gain may be assessing what's going on in your relationship. Retake the *Dating Litmus Test* to find out whether your score has decreased in inverse proportion to his weight gain.

Sometimes, weight gain simply sneaks up on a guy. Men who were skinny throughout their teenage years and young adulthood may not be used to the idea that they can put on pounds. They carry on their adolescent eating habits, drinking soda, snacking on candy bars, eating burgers and fries on their lunch break, and downing a couple of beers a night. As young men they were accustomed to burning calories at a high rate, so these habits didn't lead to much weight gain. Now that their metabolism has slowed down from age and decreased activity, they find themselves needing larger jeans and a little discipline to keep the problem from getting worse.

Even if your man seems perfectly content with your relationship and the state of his body, are you? My wife and I are both extremely fit, and I can honestly tell you that I learned early in life that I could not be with someone who let her body go. I come from a Greek household where food is god. There were many family members from older generations who were obese and suffered related health problems as a result. Their difficulties remain a huge motivation for me to stay in shape, and to have a partner who feels the same way.

I think before two people commit to spending their life together, they need to know their physical hot buttons—for example, what they can and can't tolerate in their partner's appearance. I have always preferred petite women. My wife is 110 pounds soaking wet, even after birthing two children in two years. Our friends ask how she recovered her figure, and I joke that I rented a Stair Master in the maternity ward and had her climbing away while the babies were napping… In reality, it was a combination of good genes and her commitment to take care of her figure. It was something that mattered to her, and she knew it mattered greatly to me.

At this point, you may be thinking of how busy your man has been and telling yourself, give the poor guy a break! He just doesn't have the time. That's not a good excuse. I was a workaholic in the tumultuous high-technology industry of Silicon Valley for more than twenty years. I worked obscene hours, sometimes more than eighty hours a week, and traveled more than 70 percent of the time, mostly out of the country. Yet I remained fit and worked out regularly. Keeping active helped me maintain my sanity, keep a competitive edge, combat stress, and refresh myself. I also took some pride in my appearance. With my family history, the odds weren't exactly in my favor.

If the man you adore falls prey to significant weight gain, what are you to do? You can encourage a more disciplined diet and exercise regimen, taking the time to educate him on eating properly. You can remind him of the activities you used to enjoy together and make plans for walks in the woods, rejoining the racquetball league, or mountain biking with his buddies. Sorry, gals—billiards, bowling, and poker don't count!

If you have good communication, you might reveal to him carefully that his weight is a turn-off, but chances are it's more effective to discuss the long-term health implications of his weight gain. You can let him know that you don't want him to suffer later on, and you don't want to lose him to an early death.

If you live together or share meals often at your home or his, plan a low-calorie and low-fat menu. Curtail wasteful calories in alcohol, soft drinks, and high-calorie desserts. Use olive or healthy vegetable oils instead of butter, cream sauces, and other saturated fats. Tempt him with fruits, vegetables, and low-fat proteins such as chicken, fresh fish, or soy.

Another promising tactic is to be a good example. He may be intimidated if you look great and he's getting bigger and softer. Use his self-consciousness to motivate him, not insult him. Invite him along on your workouts. Let him witness the accolades bestowed by friends or acquaintances, and maybe his sense of self-respect and competition will motivate him to get back in shape.

Note: If your partner is struggling with an illness such as a thyroid condition or diabetes, is injured or on medication, or is dealing with other significant challenges that may affect his physical condition, remember to be patient. You may not be able to help him reverse his weight gain right away.

Some people, men and women, say it's far too tough to remain disciplined 24/7, but I counter that position with the argument that you only need to be strong a few hours per day.

• While shopping, buy only healthy, low-calorie foods with less than 30 percent fat calories.

• When choosing a restaurant, avoid fast-food chains, junk-food restaurants, and other places where fried entrées and sweets rule the menu.

• Before a meal, curtail unnecessary carbohydrates in accompaniments, such as bread and butter or chips and salsa.

• After finishing the main course, just say no to the dessert menu.

• When offered food at work or at another's home, refuse high-calorie offerings.

• Limit snacks to fruits and vegetables or other-low calorie, low-fat alternatives.

• When at the bar, limit the beer and other cocktails.

A few additional health tips:

• Eat most of your meals at home, where you can control the ingredients.

• When ordering at a restaurant, don't be shy about asking for customized meals or getting information about how meals are prepared. Some simple examples:

—Request dressings or toppings on the side.

—Ask that vegetables be steamed instead of sautéed in butter.

—Order marinara sauce instead of a heavy cream-based sauce.

—Request food prepared with olive or vegetable oil instead of lard or butter.

• Read up on healthy diet plans.

• Check with a physician or nutritionist to ensure that your diet is sustainable, particularly if weight loss is a driving force.

If You're Trying to Make It Work Out with The Triathlete:

There's hope if...

✳ You can agree on what you can and can't tolerate in each other's physical condition.

✳ He welcomes your efforts to encourage healthy eating and exercise.

✳ You share at least some common interests in physical activities and diet.

✳ He's aware he's gotten out of shape and is making some effort to take better care of himself.

✳ He is getting regular medical checkups (where his doc should give him a wake-up call about the hazards of his condition).

✳ His personality, demeanor, sex drive, energy level, and professional ambition aren't compromised as a result of weight gain.

Ditch him if...

✳ He is hostile to the idea of taking better care of himself, and rebels by increasing his bad habits.

✳ You are no longer physically attracted to him.

✳ His life is spiraling down a path of decadence, almost as if he wants to do damage to himself, without being aware of the impact his attitude has on others (namely you).

✳ He becomes a bad influence on you, since you have your own problems with discipline.

✳ His complacency about his condition has hurt other aspects of his life, such as his career.

✳ He has become a different person, and you have fallen out of love with him.

Profile 10:
Mr. Heavy Baggage

O N ONE OF YOUR FIRST dates, you were moved by the way he opened up to you. He shared stories from his past until late into the night. Many of those stories weren't pretty. He spoke of his neglectful mother and his scornful father, his underprivileged childhood, friends and teachers who didn't understand him. Then there were the girlfriends who tore his heart in two. He doesn't leave out The Evil Ex-Wife, a woman who dragged him into almost inconceivable depths of misery with her lying, cheating, abusive, and angry ways. He may even have suffered through mental, physical, or sexual abuse.

He speaks of these old disappointments as if the wounds were still fresh. He asks you to avoid wearing a certain shade of lipstick, because it was similar to what his ex used. When he hears a song popular when he was a child, he grows quiet, his sadness visible on his face. When you ask him what's wrong, though, he'll readily talk, mulling over the details of his past with a thoroughness that comes from years of expensive therapy. He tells you frequently what a good listener you are.

He often blames his shortcomings—temper, moodiness,

habitual tardiness, or general unhappiness—on what he refers to as his "issues." You try to be understanding, but sometimes you can't help but feel he should live in the present, not his past.

Meet Mr. Heavy Baggage. He may be sensitive and thoughtful. He may be a deep thinker. He may be kind. You may be attracted to him because he's so different from other men, who don't seem to want to show emotion or vulnerability. But it's hard to watch him be so weighed down by his past. Difficult memories take up so much space in his head you're not sure if there's really room for you.

Mr. Heavy Baggage may always use his past to explain his present. He can't relax at work because he once had an unreasonable boss who fired him, causing him to feel like a failure. He can't trust people because a friend once betrayed him. Love relationships, of course, can be particularly fraught. He's always wary—that you'll betray him like his wife did, ignore him like his mother did, or insult him like his father did.

A different type of Mr. Heavy Baggage may keep everything bottled up inside. You may run into vast inconsistencies or big personality shifts and not understand why. Eventually, his past surfaces, and many of the behavioral patterns make better sense. He may have kept his history quiet out of fear of scaring you off. He could be in denial. He might even suffer from repressed memory syndrome and be unable to recall traumatic events earlier in his life. In these cases, you face the challenge of trying to learn more about his life and discover why he acts the way he does.

A woman in college dated this seemingly fantastic guy, and they got serious quickly. She moved in with him within six months, and in year two they discussed marriage plans. They appeared to have a wonderful relationship until one night, they had a horrible fight. He hit her, closed fist in the face.

They broke up immediately. The full story finally surfaced months later. As a child, he'd witnessed his father beating his mother. Somehow, when he was pushed to the limit, this bad instinct overtook him and he responded violently, forever changing both his and his prior girlfriend's lives. As a child, he was not provided any counseling; as an adult, he had to live with the consequences.

How can you know if your man is dealing with such extremely heavy baggage? You may get some idea by learning what you can about his family. If all the children are estranged from his father, you need to ask why. I must caution you, however, that just because someone has a bad parent or relative doesn't necessarily mean that he or she is a bad person or will exhibit the same behavior.

See the *"Are You in an Abusive Relationship?"* section in *Profile 8: The Man in Control* for more information on what to do if your man lashes out at you, verbally or physically.

If your guy is contending with past trauma, the bottom line is: Can he really get close to you, or has his past wounded him too deeply? How do you feel about coping with so much emotional turmoil? Could his rooted problems eventually become a serious problem for you or a potential family?

Another kind of Mr. Heavy Baggage out there is a man with a mental or developmental disorder (see "*When Something About Him Doesn't Seem Quite Right*"). Millions of Americans have such disorders. Many of them seek treatment and live fulfilling lives, with professional success, close personal relationships, and financial stability. Others don't get sufficient care or aren't motivated enough to overcome the obstacles their disorder throws in their way.

Loving a man with such a disorder requires patience above and beyond what's normally required in relationships. You may need to wait out difficult periods. You may need to understand that he can't endure the same amount of socializing or level of activity that you can. You may be exposed to social embarrassment if your man's on a manic streak, or is struck with phobias or compulsions that others may not readily understand.

You need to be honest with yourself. Can you handle it? Or will you resent him for the ways he isn't "normal"? Will you resent yourself for being a martyr or a free "shrink on demand"? What if you have a disorder of your own? Does that increase the risk of a problematic relationship?

You must ask yourself whether he's holding up his end. Is he going to a good doctor and taking care of himself? Is he taking the proper medications? Does he use his disorder as a crutch or an excuse for anything that doesn't go his way? Or is he determined not to let his disorder stand in his way? Will his illness restrict you in professional, personal, or financial prosperity? Is his disorder genetic, thereby placing any offspring at risk of inheriting it?

If You Think You Can Handle Mr. Heavy Baggage:

There's hope if...

✳ He's getting therapy and communicating with you on his progress.

✳ He doesn't need to withdraw from you for too long before he regains his equilibrium.

✳ His past hasn't prevented him from working and maintaining strong relationships with family, friends, and colleagues.

✳ He doesn't blame his disorder or difficult past on you or others who weren't involved.

✳ He takes care of himself, with the proper medications and routine, to prevent depression and meltdowns.

✳ He sees his heavy baggage as a challenge to overcome.

Ditch him if...

✳ You cannot tolerate his condition.

✳ He turns his problems in your problems.

✳ You feel threatened by his violent mood swings.

✳ You feel like you're constantly "walking on eggshells," watching what you do and say so you don't trigger his rage or depression, worsen his condition, or remind him of a past event.

✳ Conversation routinely regresses to his past or his mental condition, with little time spent talking about anything else.

✳ He blames everything on his past or his condition.

When Something About Him Doesn't Seem Quite Right...
Symptoms of Common Disorders

Disorder	Symptom
Anxiety Disorder	Inability to control excessive anxiety and worry for a sustained period of time, with related difficulties in sleeping, concentration, mood swings, and energy levels
Attention Deficit Disorder	Difficulty paying attention or getting work done; avoiding tasks requiring concentration; disorganization; forgetfulness; fidgeting; procrastination (4%–6% of U.S., or 12–18 million people). Usually persists throughout lifetime; one-half to two-thirds of children carry into adulthood.

Asperger's Syndrome	Impaired ability to interact socially; preoccupation with certain areas of interest or expertise; adherence to specific, nonfunctional routines or rituals; repetitive or clumsy motor mannerisms; one of several autism spectrum disorders (http://en.wikipedia.org/wiki/Autism_spectrum).
Bipolar disorder	Extreme changes in mood, thought, energy, and behavior; alternating poles of manic "highs" and depressive "lows"
Borderline Personality Disorder	Instability in personal relationships and self-image; impulsivity; self-destructive behavior; rages; stress-related paranoia
Depression (clinical)	Persistent sadness; lack of pleasure; sleep problems; loss of appetite, inability to concentrate; feelings of worthlessness, helplessness, and hopelessness

Obsessive Compulsive Disorder (OCD)	Recurrent unwanted and intrusive thoughts (obsessions) and/or repetitive behaviors (compulsions or "rituals")
Panic Disorder	Overtaken by sudden surges of overwhelming fear without warning and obvious reason, often with physical symptoms, such as chest pains, racing heartbeat, or chills
Post-Traumatic Stress Disorder	Recurrent, distressing recollections of a traumatic event; feeling or acting as if the event were recurring; intense psychological distress when exposed to reminders of the event
Social Phobias	Marked and persistent fear of certain social or performance situations that may expose the person to unfamiliar people or scrutiny by others

Profile 11:
The Older Man

ELEBRITIES DO IT. THERE'S ANNA Nicole Smith, who married oil businessman and billionaire J. Howard Marshall, 63 years her senior. Michael Douglas is 25 years older than wife Catherine Zeta-Jones. George Clooney always has a much younger hottie on his arm.

As glamorous as falling in love with an older man may seem, my advice is to tread carefully and know what you are in for in the long haul. The dashing older man who sweeps you off your feet today may, in the not-too-distant future, lose his looks and depend on you as his chauffeur and personal care assistant.

I think it's a fact that men mature later than women, particularly in affairs of the heart. Women often find men their own age ill-prepared for relationships and not yet established professionally or financially. Older men may be more secure and know more about how to please a woman, physically and emotionally. Women may gravitate to men who have fatherly qualities, like those of their own dad, or characteristics they wish their old man possessed.

You may want the financial security of being with a man who owns his home and has a nest egg. Perhaps you've struggled through the routine of living paycheck to paycheck, or have bitter memories from an underprivileged childhood. You want a different future. You want to raise children and not have to work outside the home.

Or perhaps you are drawn to older men with distinction and power, as is an East Coast woman I know. She's an attorney who's very active politically and socially in high-society circles. Throughout her thirties and into her forties, she routinely dated men more than twenty years her senior. Raising a family was never a priority for her. Now in her mid-forties, she recently settled down with a man in his late sixties. They are happy, but she's come to realize that she may have limited years of quality time with her man. She's also confronting the realization that she may spend the last twenty years or more of her life without him, and without any children or grandchildren. It's a sacrifice she's decided to accept.

Can you?

You may love him now, and you certainly appreciate the benefits of being with an older, wiser, worldly, and more financially stable man. You are willing to compromise other ideals you may have about his appearance, physical condition, and ability to enjoy common interests. But you also need to ask yourself: What will life be like in ten years? Twenty? Thirty? While your friends are looking forward to an active early retirement in their sixties, will you be faced with changing the diapers of an incontinent man in his eighties?

I am not against older men. In fact, I am one and I'd always thought I'd be one. When I was in my late twenties to early thirties, I used to joke when friends asked me when I was going to marry that "my wife is still struggling with trigonometry." I did end up marrying someone ten years younger. Ginger probably was having her share of difficulties in mathematics when I was addressing these queries.

I have been fortunate to maintain a fairly youthful appearance, looking five or more years younger than my natural age. Fortunately or unfortunately, my wife looks even younger for her age. Once while we were dating and out golfing, a ranger asked me if she was my daughter! Granted, she was wearing a baseball cap, and, while nearly thirty, looked nineteen. I was approaching forty.

If you're dating an older man, it's important to think through all the implications of sharing a future together, particularly if the age difference is greater than fifteen years—the kind of gap that typically inspires the "he's old enough to be your father" line. Women have a longer average life expectancy than men, and life expectancy goes up from generation to generation. According to statistics from the Centers for Disease Control, a woman born in 1970 has an average life expectancy of 74.6 years, while a man born in 1950 has an average life expectancy of 65.5 years. That means she faces a statistical likelihood of living nearly thirty years after he dies—quite a long widowhood.

Also consider the *relative age* of your older man. Assessing a wide variety of factors—physical fitness, cholesterol levels, family history (is longevity in his genes?)—can help you determine whether you are with a fifty-year-old man with the body of a forty-year-old or your guy is physically older than his years indicate.

Relative age explains why, at your twentieth high school reunion, there's such a wide variation in how old people look. As you greet your old friends with, "Hey! What have you been up to over all these years?" you may be thinking, "Holy sh__, I went to high school with this guy and he looks like he could be my father!" or "Wow, she doesn't look like she just raised a family, she appears to have eaten them too! She's enormous." Then, of course, there's that geeky girl from the debate team who, thanks to a great career and healthy living, glows like a college sophomore.

You may want to compare your relative age to your man's. There's an excellent test on (http://www.RealAge.com) that estimates relative age from information about your general health, medical history, prescription medications, lifestyle and safety habits, nutrition, physical activity, stress, and social support systems. You may discover, to your delight, that your fifty-year-old sweetie has the body of a forty-two-year-old. Or you may have to face the implications of being with a man whose body is aging even faster than he is, which may mean a caretaking period and/or widowhood that are even longer than you'd anticipated.

If you are in love with The Older Man, you need to ask yourself:

• How do you feel about the possibility that he won't be able to share the same activities with you once you hit fifty or so? He may no longer be up to a tennis match, ambitious vacation travel, or even going out to dinner after six.

• Does he have more in common with your parents than with yourself?

• Are you finding any of his mores "old-fashioned"?

• What about your sex life? His functioning and drive will probably diminish long before yours does.

• Does he want to father children? Will he change diapers at sixty? Coach youth soccer at seventy?

• If he already has kids, will it be awkward being a step-mother to someone not much younger than you are?

• Do you constantly get the impression that he thinks he knows better than you?

• Does he have respect for your career or personal aspirations?

• Are there any generational gaps that you are starting to find annoying?

—Gender roles

—Health- or diet-related issues

—Interests in music, books, culture, or activities

—Technology (he's awkward with the computer, Internet, DVR, iPod)

• Can you maintain the patience to take care of him as he ages? Can you face the possibility of physical handicaps and a dimmed intellect?

One woman reported her experience with dating older men, whom she found incredibly "world weary" and disillusioned; they wanted a younger woman to renew their spirits. This solution was only temporary, and they returned to their bitter demeanor.

Not every Older Man will have a tainted view on life, but some will have spent years alone, experienced great loss (of a loved one), or had several disappointing relationships. They may have been hardened by these personal experiences.

If you're enjoying a fulfilling relationship with an older man, you may find this section discouraging. I'm not trying to tell you to automatically ditch The Older Man; I'm just encouraging you to think through all of the implications, now and in the future. Picture how your relationship will evolve over time. Imagine your life together in ten years, twenty years, and beyond. What do you see? Are you happy?

If You're Considering a Future with The Older Man:

There's hope if...
✳ You have many common interests, despite the age difference.
✳ You can look into the future unafraid of the prospect

that he may become frail, disabled, or no longer interested in sex (or even impotent) years before you are.

✳ You are willing to remain loyal and care for him as he ages.

✳ He understands and appreciates that your circle of friends will likely include people closer to your age.

✳ You are at peace, realizing that this is the man that you truly love, and spending a fixed amount of time with him now is worth the loss and loneliness you may feel in the future.

Ditch him if...

✳ You are with him only for the financial security.

✳ He is condescending to you and your friends.

✳ You're disgusted by the thought of being stuck with an old man who requires your care.

✳ You've assessed your relative age versus his on (http://www.RealAge.com), and the results make you cringe with dread.

✳ You can't accept that you may need to be a nursemaid to this man.

Profile 12:
The Younger Man

WHILE SOME WOMEN GRAVITATE TOWARD the maturity and security The Older Man may offer, others may not be able to resist the allure of The Younger Man.

What's not to love? His body is more muscular, and his face is less wrinkled. His sense of the future is more open and optimistic. He goes bungee jumping and plays paint ball. His iPod is full of the latest tunes from Gnarls Barkley and M.I.A. He's energetic and spontaneous. His vigor and stamina is more than apparent in the bedroom.

Older Woman/Younger Man matchups aren't as common as Older Man/Younger Woman pairs. There's a something of a social stigma, as men are assumed to want a younger women's figure, natural beauty, and aura, while women are supposed to desire an older man's maturity, status, and wealth.

But The Younger Man has his own kind of status. He can make you feel sexier and carefree. He shows well on your shoulder when you're out in public. He may not expect as much from you. He may be more relaxed about his career, family planning, or purchasing a home. If you're uncertain about any of these endeavors yourself, dating The Younger Man buys you time. But it would be wise to ask yourself what will happen when you do become more certain about what you want in life. Will he still be holding on to his foot-loose lifestyle?

In The Older Man, I presented the idea of relative age—how the life expectancy for a woman is typically longer than for a man, so the age gap may feel even bigger than it really is (especially if The Older Man has bad habits and doesn't take care of himself properly). With The Younger Man, you may theoretically be closer in relative age, but you're faced with another, perhaps more daunting, problem: relative *maturity*.

You've known since elementary school that girls mature faster than boys. They develop language skills earlier, sit still sooner, and hit puberty well before the boys. As I've discussed, women are typically ready to settle down and bear children earlier, as they have their biological clocks to consider.

So if you are looking for a life partner and the father of your children, you need to ask yourself whether The Younger Man is really ready for the same things. Will he be mature enough to be a dad when you're ready to be a mom?

It's also important to ask yourself: Are your goals in life and *your timeline for achieving them* compatible? If he wants to start a restaurant, but he's still spinning dough at the local pizzeria, will his plans (or yours) be stymied if you're thirty-five and you know you want to have a child in the next three years?

Trust is another huge matter. Dating an older woman may feel exotic to him now, but is he the kind of man you can depend on to stay faithful and interested as you age and your appearance loses its youthfulness, as it inevitably will? Or will you be scurrying to the plastic surgeon every year in an effort to try to look like women his age?

If you are a woman with a high-powered career and substantial assets, keep in mind that he may be looking at you as aficionados of The Older Man look at their catch: a way to access wealth, security, and comfort. If so, will you resent him for depending on you? Will he resent you for being the breadwinner? You may want to review *Profile 6: The Under-achiever.*

The age difference is less critical for couples who don't want children and share a lot in common. A woman finally married her longtime partner. She was a blushing bride at fifty-three; he was forty. Neither wants children, and they run a successful business together.

They are happy. Still, with an age gap like that, crucial questions remain. What will happen to their sex life when he's not yet sixty and she's entering her seventies? Can she depend on him if she becomes ill or infirm while he's still active?

If you're facing these questions, you may not know the answers until you get there. But if the age gap is more than five or ten years, you'll want to have a serious discussion with your man about these matters. You'll need to tackle some of the difficult questions:

- Are you on a similar professional trajectory?
  —You may be "settled" in your career.
  —He may still be in the early stages or searching for direction.
- Is there an imbalance in financial contributions?
- Is there "substance" after the initial aesthetic or physical connection?
- Are there any signs of generational incompatibilities?
- Is he your intellectual equal?
- Will you be sexually compatible in five, ten, or twenty years?
  —What happens if one loses sex drive much earlier?
  —Can you depend upon him if your health declines?

If The Younger Man Puts a Spring in Your Step:

There's hope if...

＊ His maturity level makes the age gap feel smaller, not larger.

＊ He's independently successful and financially well off.

＊ Your family planning goals are compatible.

＊ You feel the thrill of attracting a younger man, but your connection is clearly much deeper.

✳ He has the opportunity to date contemporaries or younger women, but has selected you.

Ditch him if...

✳ He's constantly checking out other women, especially younger ones, as if longing for a match closer to his own age.

✳ You're attracted to him sexually, but you don't have much else in common.

✳ He criticizes your shape, or has hinted more than once that you should get cosmetic improvements.

✳ You get the impression that he's taking advantage of you.

✳ He tells you he's not nearly ready to be a father, and you're approaching the end of your optimal child-bearing years.

Profile 13:
The Wannabe

MANY PEOPLE ARE STAR-CRAZED, PARTICULARLY women. They consume one gossip magazine after another and surf online for the latest celebrity news. They watch the talk shows and the entertainment channel. They're hungry to learn about the latest celebrity faux pas and scandalous Hollywood couple breakup. They want to see that gorgeous—or embarrassing—paparazzi photograph. On Oscar night, viewers are usually more intent on getting a glimpse of the celebrities than they are on finding out who won the awards. They want to know what the stars are wearing, whom they're with, and what they have to say.

Americans are infatuated with celebrities of all sorts: actors, musicians, athletes, socialites, business moguls, big-time politicians. We follow their lives intently, through their peaks and valleys. We're mesmerized by the glamour of their lavish lifestyles. We're transfixed by the triumphs and tragedies of their lives.

I think that many women are so enamored with the lifestyles of the rich and famous that they look for an aura of celebrity in their significant other. They find a man who seems to have star power. Maybe it comes from his glory days gone by as the high school homecoming king. It could have derived from his certainty that his rock band, business idea, or local political campaign will make him The Next Big Thing. Could it be from all the important people he seems to know? What about the allure from being a member of one of the wealthiest or most prominent families in town?

You're not the only one who's drawn to him. His old high school buddies and girlfriends love to hang out with him, and he's still the center of attention at the local pub when he retells stories about the big game his senior year. At cocktail parties, he quickly draws an attentive audience as he brags about the big contract he's about to sign, rubbing elbows with celebrity row, or the television sitcom role he's bound to be offered.

When he turns his attention toward you, the opportunity is exciting. If he was the popular guy in high school, you're flattered to be considered worthy of his affection now. If you believe he's a rising star, dating him may mean you'll ascend along with him, as the faithful girlfriend who believed in him from the start. You may be in for a little celebrity status yourself, you think, if you stay by his side.

But before you indulge in too much daydreaming, you need to ask yourself: Is this man's importance genuine or trumped up? Is he truly respected by all those important or famous people he seems to know? Do these supposed famous people even matter to you beyond the novelty of an initial introduction?" If he's talented, has he been making progress in his chosen field, or is he still blustering on about that one bit part he had in a Robert De Niro film five years ago?

Don't get hoodwinked by a persona. No matter how enticing he seems, he still needs to pass the Dating Litmus Test. It's fine to be initially attracted to him for what he represents or once did, but you need to make sure he has depth of character and that the relationship is worth sustaining.

Is he a name-dropper, taking every opportunity to make sure everyone knows who *he* knows? Is he a story-topper, who needs every conversation to be about him and his exploits? This can be very annoying at social gatherings, when no one else really gets to talk. You may rationalize that he relishes or even deserves some attention because of his past accomplishments or future promise, but that doesn't excuse a man who's so full of himself he can't bear to let anyone else have a say.

If the guy who's entered your life hogs the spotlight, he's on a perpetual mission to prove that he's a Very Big Deal. If he really were such a hot shot, he probably wouldn't need to work so hard to prove it! Humility is a valued characteristic. These wannabes are more "sell-ebrity" than celebrity, because they're so busy selling themselves as famous and important, as opposed to actually being famous and important. Real celebrities are often somewhat reclusive, precisely because they don't need to prove themselves anymore and have actually grown weary of so much attention.

A Wannabe may be self-centered in other ways, as well. He

may not call or show up when he's supposed to, or may cancel plans at the last minute. His excuse? He's jumping at a business or professional opportunity that "suddenly came up." He probably ran into a big shot he wants to network with (read: kiss up to), or, worse, a new woman he believes is better suited to his ambitions. Often these Wannabes are making parallel commitments and taking the best offer at that moment of time, inconsiderate of anyone else's time or feelings.

Some star figures are riding success from decades earlier. Even though they haven't done much since, they've managed to build a career and income stream around past accomplishments. Some celebrities and retired pro athletes spend much of their time traveling around, performing on cruises and at resorts, giving speeches, judging contests, or golfing with generous executives. It's a great deal for them, but what about the significant other or family? If The Wannabe flits around the globe entertaining former fans, he may not ever stay still for you or the children you hope to have one day. You'll also want to ask yourself how you feel about sharing your life with a man who's spending all his time looking backward instead of moving on to new challenges.

If You Want the Wannabe to Be Yours:

There's hope if...
✳ He cherishes his past, but places more emphasis on present and future priorities.
✳ He has a practical Plan B to fall back on if he can't make it into the limelight with Plan A.

✳ He found a way to leverage his past success into present-day accomplishments (such as creating a high-end network for selling, promoting, or providing services).

✳ He enjoys rubbing elbows with the rich and famous, but hasn't lost touch with his own sense of reality.

✳ He is genuinely happy for others who achieve success, and still works hard to achieve his own goals.

Ditch him if...

✳ He often cancels at the last minute or is inappropriately late because he's posing as someone in demand.

✳ He kisses up to people with "star power" and is insincere with others he considers less useful to his interests.

✳ His prior fame makes him feel entitled to gratuities, so he rarely pays his way.

✳ He always dominates conversations because he's too egotistical to listen to others.

✳ He tries to sell himself off as someone he isn't.

Profile 14:
Mr. Inattentive

ALMOST EVERY WOMAN, AT SOME point, believes that her man suffers from some form of attention deficit disorder. He'll pick up the newspaper in the middle of your description of the latest drama at the office that day. While touring through a world-class museum, he'll start playing with his Blackberry. You want to have a talk about your relationship, and he suddenly can't put off that telephone call to his golf buddy, or he's distracted by something on TV. Then there's the classic scenario—after sex you want to cuddle and talk, but he's drifting off to sleep.

Why do guys do tune out? There's the biological reality that orgasm makes men sleepy. Beyond that, men and women have starkly different interests and look at life from vastly different perspectives. Your man might not always be able to get completely absorbed in the things you want to talk about. As traditional hunters, men naturally like to roam, and their minds do, too. As traditional caretakers of children and the home, women like to talk about relationships, be it family, romantic, or professional. Men like to "fix things," and if there isn't a quick remedy to a problem, they're likely to struggle. Women like to nurture and often want to vent, expecting their man simply to listen to what they have to say and not judge them.

So you may not need to take his wandering mind too much to heart. In most cases, all you need to do is ask firmly but politely for his attention. Explain that you really need him to focus for a few minutes, after which he's welcome to do his own thing. He may take comfort if you tell him that you only need him alert for a fixed period (more than an hour could be problematic). If he cooperates, you know that all he needed was a little wake-up call.

There's also a chance that he absorbed more than he let on. If you're not sure whether he truly heard you, refer back to something important you shared with him earlier in the conversation. Try not to obviously quiz him, as that could backfire. If he's truly clueless about what you were talking about, that's endemic of a larger problem.

Be sensitive about when you expect his full attention. A few times that may not be the best time to address concerns:

• First thing in the morning if he's not an early bird (before his coffee)
   • Late at night, once his mind has started to fade
   • After a long day at the office
   • During a bout of insomnia or when he's recovering from jet lag
   • Right after a workout or if he's missed a meal, when his blood sugar may be low

• When he's going through a tough period at work or with his family
• When he's in a rush
• When he's preparing for a test for a night class or completing a major project
• After a few cocktails or taking heavy medication
• When he's sick or really down

When a guy tunes out too often, though, you can start to feel like you are invisible or irrelevant.

You may be familiar with the following scenario: You've gotten all dolled up for dining out, and you're receiving flattering recognition from others. But your date isn't focused. He's fidgety and can't relax. He incessantly peers down at his cell phone as if he's waiting for an important text message. He takes calls in the middle of your dinner, treating you at times like you're not actually there with him. His eyes are constantly wandering, as if he's looking for someone or something better. He may even be overtly checking out other women. You try to engage him in conversation, but he doesn't give you the impression that he's paying full attention.

You go through the motions and get through the evening, wondering what the heck was up. Then he has the audacity to expect some intimacy that night! You refuse, not willing to subject yourself to further neglect.

As you reflect on the evening, you realize that his eyes and mind were in perpetual motion. He wasn't able to even make eye contact with you for longer than a few seconds. You think back to your past few dates, and you can't remember the last time you had a meaningful discussion. Every time you began a conversation, he'd wait until you finished talking, his foot tapping under the table, then bring up an entirely different topic to suit his interests. If someone asked him right after your dates what you talked about, he probably would remember only what he said, oblivious to the subjects you'd raised. Sometimes you felt like he was just passing the time until he could get you into the bedroom.

This kind of behavior cuts deeper than the "all guys have a little ADD" syndrome. There's some chance this squirmy fellow might actually have adult attention deficit disorder (more on that below), but before you try to diagnose him, consider the possibility that, wittingly or unwittingly, he's sending signals that he's not ready for a real relationship, or at least not with you.

He may just be going through the motions of intimacy. He may like the ego boost of being seen with a woman in public, creating the appearance of being an in-demand type of guy as a kind of advertising for future prospects. He may be too full of himself or too distracted by work or personal problems to focus on you. He may just want to have fun, enjoy life, and experiment. Are you experimenting, or are you uncomfortable being a specimen in his petri dish?

There's always the chance he may be holding on to the misguided grade-school wisdom that boys should ignore girls they like! In that case, the love connection just isn't going to be there—he's not up to it yet.

You may want to take note as to whether he has trouble concentrating just around you, or around everyone. It's problematic either way, of course, but at least you'll have some indication of whether he's not interested in you or self-absorbed in general.

Sometimes a guy who hangs on your every word in the first months of your courtship goes into big-time tune-out mode later on. Does he notice things about you that should be obvious? For example:

• Significant weight loss through dieting and exercising
• A dramatically shorter hairstyle or a change in the color or highlights
• A French-tips manicure
• The pair of designer shoes on which you squandered your paycheck
• A racy negligee to spice up your sex life
• New sheets or household décor
• A different shampoo, soap, or lotion
• That you now speak to him in a foreign language

Guys will often pay attention only to things that have an immediate affect on them: a new car, a comfortable chair cushion, an exotic meal. I'm positive most men would identify with some level of animation if you had a boob job!

In certain cases, you may find yourself wondering whether your man actually has a clinical problem. About half to two-thirds of children with attention deficit hyperactivity disorder (ADHD) continue to experience symptoms as adults in a disorder known as adult attention deficit disorder, in which the hyperactivity gives way to restlessness and fidgety behavior. Other symptoms commonly associated with AADD include lack of focus, disorganization, difficulty finishing projects, and a tendency to lose things. These symptoms may interfere with success at work and personal relationships, which is where you come in. Many adults remain undiagnosed and subsequently untreated. If you have concerns about your man, you should encourage a comprehensive medical diagnosis and treatment. Men who really have AADD may actually be very enthusiastic about you, but other symptoms may make an enduring relationship difficult.

A Colorado woman met a really great guy at a nightclub. They danced together until late and made plans to see each other again. After a few dates, he turned up the speed on their romance. They spent all their free time together, hiking in the mountains and going out to concerts, movies, and dinners. She met all of his close friends, and he met hers. He seemed to have boundless energy, staying up late and rising early, bright-eyed and ready for another day of falling in love. He couldn't stay still. He confessed to her that he had been diagnosed with AADD, but she didn't mind because he was so sweet and fun.

Then she began to learn more about him. He'd never held a job or an apartment for long. He'd been divorced twice. He ran his own furniture-making business on a shoestring because he never had the patience to come up with a long-term business plan. He had no health insurance, even though he was entering his fifties. He pushed her to spend more and more time with him, even when she was overwhelmed with work obligations. Friends began to confide in her that though they were happy she was in love, she also looked exhausted all the time. The relationship collapsed under the weight of his financial irresponsibility and his hot temper.

It can be difficult to sort through the many varieties of male inattention. Is it temporary and easily resolvable with a reminder or two that, hello, you're in the room too, or a sign that he's just not into the relationship? Or is it a clinical disorder?

Whatever your situation, it's important to keep in mind that if a man persists in not paying attention to you, little you do or say is going to help. He's not listening. And why do you want to be with a man who ignores you, anyway?

If You're Focusing on Mr. Inattentive:

There's hope if...
✳ When you gently suggest his mind is wandering, he apologizes profusely and makes sure to keep his eyes intently on yours for the rest of the conversation.
✳ You discover that he has a much easier time paying

attention to you in quiet surroundings—he's just one of those people who can't handle too much stimulation at once.

✳ He actually has AADD, is willing to seek treatment, *and* you're willing to accept the idiosyncrasies of he disorder.

✳ His difficulties paying attention are stress-related and he tunes in again once the tough times have passed.

✳ He's in a high-powered career that requires him to be on call much of the time, but he handles interruptions politely and makes sure to set aside time for you exclusively.

✳ He recognizes when he is distracted and asks for your understanding.

Ditch him if...

✳ He gets irritable and can't comply when you ask him to focus on what you're saying.

✳ He finds it impossible to keep his eyes on you, even during an intimate dinner.

✳ His struggle with AADD means more emotional, professional, and financial instability than you can handle.

✳ His mind and eyes are wandering because he's looking for someone more fun, more attractive, or more professionally useful.

✳ He has no ability to prioritize, taking every incoming call, e-mail, and text message with no regard to your feelings.

✳ You rarely get the feeling that you have his full attention and that he is being attentive to your needs.

Profile 15:
The Mama's Boy

Y OU'VE ALWAYS VALUED A FAMILY man. You believe a
guy who has a close relationship to his own parents
has tons of dad potential. And a man who treats his
mother well is bound to know how to honor and respect
women.

But there's a downside. That faithful son you're getting
to know sometimes seems a little too devoted. He calls his
mother every day to share the details of his professional and
personal life. Weekends often include a visit to his parents.
His mother dotes on him with food and attention in a way
that is both sweet and intimidating. She's nice to you, but
also a bit guarded. You've even felt at times that you are in
direct competition with her for his affection.

You're dating a Mama's Boy. This can be good news if
she likes you and treats you well. If she approves of you as
a daughter once your relationship with her son gets serious, even better. If you accept her, she could become a close
friend, confidante, and future babysitter. Many cultures encourage this kind of bond between mother and daughter-in-
law. The relationship doesn't have to be fraught, even if your
man and his mama are closer than you'd prefer.

But there can definitely be real tension between a Mama's Boy's mama and his significant other. You may feel slighted that he shares so much with his mother. She seems to always come first, leaving you feeling like the second fiddle. Other danger signals include:

- He hints—or flat-out tells you—that no one will ever compare to her.
- He is always making compromises or sacrifices to accommodate her.
- He still observes his mother's religion or cultural traditions to placate her.
- He has secrets and inside jokes with his mother that make you feel like an outsider.
- He can't make important decisions without her input.
- He requires her validation of major accomplishments.
- He lives with her.
- He is financially dependent on her.

It is not fun having your man's mother overshadow your life. The situation may put overt or covert pressure on you to be like her, even if your life is nothing like hers.

Take a successful advertising executive who is in a relationship with a slightly younger man who works as a part-time chef. He is close to his parents. Whenever she has time off from work, he drags her to his parents' cabin, where his mother spoils him with cooking and attention. She despises these trips, but goes along rather than face the ramifications if she refuses. Although she is a take-charge woman at the office, she becomes subservient at home. She cooks, cleans, and caters to her man, just like his mother did.

The situation can get toxic if your man's mother actively meddles in your life and his. A meddling mama may show the following characteristics:

• She tries to get involved in your day-to-day affairs.
• She critiques the way you look, dress, cook, and clean.
• She rarely compliments you.
• She picks fights, particularly when company's around, and often at events you're hosting.
• She never bothers to make you feel comfortable in her home.
• She gossips about you behind your back, then denies it when confronted.
• She makes it abundantly clear that no woman is good enough for her son.

If you marry this man, his meddling mama will likely become the mother-in-law from hell. Her criticisms will extend to your housekeeping and how you raise your children. You'll prefer to pay a stranger to babysit rather than call her, because you know she'll wipe her finger over your dresser to check for dust and look through your pantry for foods she would never be caught dead serving.

Even if you can tolerate his mother for brief intervals, you need to think about what will happen if she takes ill and your man doesn't want to leave her alone. How will you feel if she moves in with him, or relocates to be closer? Before committing to him for the long term, you'll need to talk about what kinds of arrangements you could tolerate. Make sure he is able to hear out your concerns without getting overly insistent or defensive. He should be looking out for everyone's best interests, not just his mother's. He needs to think first about himself, you, and your future children, if you're planning to have them together.

If You're Attached to The Mama's Boy...

There's hope if...
* You really like his mom and enjoy spending time with her.
* His mom lives far away and you won't have to deal with her idiosyncrasies very often.
* You like the idea of becoming a part of a close-knit family.
* As you get closer to him, he gradually takes your advice into account as much as he does his mother's.
* He makes it clear there's plenty of room in his life for you.
* He will defend you overtly if his mom attacks, particularly in your own home.

Ditch him if...
* He lives with his parents in a small (read: no room for you) residence and never wants to move out.
* He insists he needs to keep you a secret from his mother because you're not part of his family's religion or ethnicity.

✳ He shares vital details of his life with his mother before sharing them with you.

✳ He seeks his mother's advice on everything and dismisses your input if it contradicts hers.

✳ He regularly cancels plans at the last minute to tend to his mother's needs, even if the reasons don't seem that urgent.

✳ He seems more interested in being coddled like a child than in having one.

Cleaning Up His Act: A Quick Guide

The Mama's Boy may come with the additional quirk of being messy or disorganized, basically because his mother picked up after him and managed his affairs all his life. He's not the only type of guy who has these flaws; I would guess a healthy majority of women would say that their men lack good housekeeping and organization habits. This problem can be extremely frustrating, and probably seems inconsiderate.

Here are some tips for countering his behavior without causing a world war. Break your man in early. Otherwise you'll either assume these duties or live with his idiosyncrasies for the next thirty to fifty years, like many of our moms did. It wasn't enough to cook and clean for their kids; they also inherited a perpetual adolescent called a husband!

✳ If you can't agree on dividing chores and can afford to contract house cleaning and yard work, do so.

✳ Establish minimal standards, such as putting away perishables, rinsing toothpaste out of the sink after brushing, and wiping the mud off shoes.

✳ Make it clear you expect him to pick up after himself.

✳ Almost every man requires reminders about placing the toilet seat down.

✳ Do laundry separately.

✳ Men may need to be told that certain items (decorative towels or soap) are for show, not practical use.

✳ Designate an out-of-the-way area for his clutter (newspapers, magazines, take-home work).

✳ Set aside a convenient drawer for his wallet, keys, money, pens, jewelry, or other trinkets.

✳ If he's reluctant to take his turn shopping, give him a grocery list.

✳ To encourage him to cook, ask him to make something he likes to eat.

✳ If he doesn't know how to cook at all, prepare new recipes together.

✳ If he drinks directly from a container, buy him his own and request that shared items be poured.

✳ Guys often think a morning shower means they're good for the day. Remind him he'll need another after golf or a walk on a warm night.

✳ Gently suggest hygiene improvements. Joke, for example, that "trimming and mowing" (getting rid of unattractive facial or body hair) isn't just for women!

✳ If he has no fashion sense, buy him clothes he looks and feels good in.

✳ If you share a car, install a bin especially for his stuff so he doesn't use the entire interior as his portable filing cabinet

✳ Arrange for him to have automatic bill payments, with deductions from his checking account.

✳ Show him how to program an electronic calendar on his computer, cell phone, or PDA, with automatic e-mail or text-message reminders of appointments, dates, birthdays, anniversaries, and holidays.

✳ On important occasions, reinforce these reminders with Post-It notes and personal e-mails and text messages.

✳ If he habitually screws up the configurations on your TV remote, alarm clock, computer, or printer, affix instructions nearby on how to return them to the proper state.

✳ Set designated locations (hooks, cubbies, drawers) for items to which you both need access, such as car and house keys.

Profile 16:
Mr. Reinvention

A MUSIC WRITER IN NEW YORK City fell in love with a musician. He had a good reputation and scored plenty of gigs as a session guitarist. Then, out of the blue, he auditioned for a role in a musical in London. He got the lead and spent several months in the spotlight in England, living large and going out to pubs every night, while she waited for him back home. He returned after the show's run ended, but he'd lost ground in the music world and his acting career fizzled.

They married and had a son. He became a stay-at-home dad while she worked long hours as an editor for a leading music magazine. He went back to work for a few years as a preschool teacher, but left to devote his energy to his latest dream—creating a new children's television show. It's clearly a gamble and unclear if or when the show will be picked up or make any money. But every time his wife suggests he might look for better-compensated work, he accuses her of not supporting his dreams. As she works late into the night, earning money to support the family, all she can think is, "I've been supporting your dreams ever since I met you. They just keep changing."

Meet Mr. Reinvention. He's a dreamer, but the moment one dream starts to come true, he gets caught up in a new one. He's ambitious, but unwilling to sustain his achievements in one area for too long. His résumé is a jumble of different jobs, often without a logical progression. After his dot-com flounders, he may work the cash register at Barnes & Noble, then land a manager trainee gig at an upscale clothing chain. He may have a blank year or two, because he'd decided the time was right to join an ashram or devote a year to writing science fiction.

He may adapt a new persona with each new endeavor. He's clean-shaven and amenable as he begins his climb up the corporate ladder, then he grows his hair and dons loose, flowing clothing for his new "true calling" as the groundskeeper for a New Age retreat center.

Mr. Reinvention may be a true seeker, still trying to figure out what it means to follow his bliss in a world where so many of us too readily sacrifice happiness for stability. He's certainly not boring. He learns quickly and adapts readily. He's probably one of the more enthusiastic travelers you know. You may get the feeling that he's having so much fun that he might not be on the return flight with you when the trip's concluded (and maybe you are wishing that he's not).

But can Mr. Reinvention help you follow *your* bliss? If he's not sticking with anything long enough to achieve lasting success, he may depend on you for financial and emotional stability. He may be needy, requiring your support for every new project, no matter how impractical. He may expect you to sustain him even as he backs out of plans on which he'd worked so hard.

You may also experience frustration with his lack of focus or his inability to pull his weight around the household. If he raised outside funding for his ventures and wasn't able to provide tangible returns, he may have estranged friends, business contacts, and family members in addition to debt.

If he's changing personas along with his professions, you may simply find that the man you thought you loved has transformed himself too drastically for your tastes. And, of course, you may wonder whether one day you'll be cast off as easily as his last abandoned pursuit.

If Mr. Reinvention Is Your Latest Project:

There's hope if...
  ✳ You love his core personality and aren't bothered by all the other changes in his life.
  ✳ He's kept steady friendships and family ties.
  ✳ He contributes where and when he can to make life easier, and you don't consider him a burden.
  ✳ His failed endeavors have not resulted in any mounting debt or bad will, either with personal or professional contacts for you both.
  ✳ He makes a genuine effort to succeed, and is passionate about each new business opportunity that arises.

＊ You aren't alienated by his financial and professional instability.

Ditch him if...
＊ He resents your success and stability.

＊ You find his demands for your support and his fiscal irresponsibility unreasonable.

＊ You don't like the new person he's become.

＊ His dreams are impractical and selfish, and he has no timetable for pursuing a more rational career path.

＊ He has little to show for his efforts, and you find it hard to respect him or not consider him a perpetual failure.

＊ He's a poor role model for potential children.

Profile 17:
The Mooch

Y OU PROBABLY DATED HIM IN college: the guy who never had any money. He was always down to his last dollar, and his ATM card mysteriously worked at only his hometown credit union, a couple of hundred miles away. You picked up the tab for burgers and the movies and pretended not to mind when he failed to buy a single tank of gas on your spring-break road trip. After a few months of this, though, you got a little resentful. Was he taking advantage of your generosity?

Not every woman needs a man with lots of money. Some women take pleasure in sharing expenses and taking turns picking up the tab, as it appeals to their sense of independence. You may not even mind a man who needs to lean on you from time to time because of temporary unemployment or a dip in cash flow. You appreciate his gratitude and hope that, if needed, he would one day do the same for you. Another scenario may be that you come from an affluent household, while his family may have struggled.

You may also meet a man who is in transition. He may be finishing a higher degree or taking time out to get certified in a skill that will increase his market value. He may be taking care of an ill family member. He may be wrapped up volunteering for a political campaign or doing charitable work. If he's a terrific guy who, for a certain period of time, doesn't have a lot of money to spend on you, you might be sorry if you turn your back because he can't pick up the tab at your favorite restaurant.

But if you find yourself called on to foot the bill too often, under conditions that seem suspect, you may be dating The Mooch. If you're not careful, the few bucks you paid for burgers and movie tickets back at school could balloon into thousands of dollars, making a real dent in your personal finances.

A successful marketing professional in California met a seemingly affluent man who worked in website development just as the Internet was starting to take off in the mid-1990s. He moved in with her after years of dating, as she owned her own home and he had been house-sitting for a wealthy friend.

The man was investing heavily in a new venture, with money borrowed from local banks, venture capitalists, friends, and family. Unbeknownst to his girlfriend, he was leveraged to the hilt and letting his lucrative website business slide. She did notice that he contributed nothing toward household expenses, and that she always had to pay the tab when they went out.

She eventually faced the fact that she was fully supporting him, financially and emotionally. Meanwhile, he was sinking deeper and deeper into debt instead of cutting his losses and taking a job as an engineer (the field he trained for) with guaranteed compensation. She realized she had to end the relationship.

Is your man:
• Pushing you to move in together prematurely, to save on expenses (namely his)?
• Pressuring you to go in on an investment with him?
• Always asking friends for money, a place to live, or a job?
• Constantly seeking out new people who can help him out?
• Given to somewhat dicey money habits?
• He pays for meals for a group of people with his credit card, then takes everyone's cash.
• He accepts receipts for everything, even if you pay, and uses them to claim business expenses.
• He screens calls from creditors.
• He has no clue as to how to balance his checking account.

Moving in together mainly for financial reasons is always a bad idea. If you think you may be ready to take the plunge, try spending time at each other's homes for extended periods. Gauge how comfortable the situation is. Honestly assess whether living together only increases his opportunities to mooch off of you—especially if he would be moving into your home.

You should maintain your financial independence as long as possible. It's best to wait to combine finances until after marriage. If you want to go ahead with an investment beforehand, make sure to have a good contract. Use an attorney who represents your interests exclusively. Your partner should hire his own representation as well. Keep in mind that if you break up, the emotional strife will be exacerbated by the financial stress of dividing joint investments, especially if he tries to hide or run off with the money.

There's no harm in dating a guy who spends a lot of time networking. It's a sign he's trying to better himself, and that's particularly important if he's out of work or trying to start a business. But a mooch networks with an anxious edge. Does he genuinely want to connect with other people, or is he just using others for personal benefit? Is he interested only in people who have a high net worth? Does he complain about (or refuse to attend) events that show little promise of personal gain, such as family birthday gatherings and dinners with friends who aren't wealthy or important?

"The true measure of a man is how he treats someone who can do him absolutely no good."
—Samuel Johnson

As you evaluate whether your man is a Mooch, keep in mind that every man forgets his wallet from time to time. But pay careful attention to how he handles the lapse. Best-case scenario: He's humiliated and offers to reimburse you as soon as he can. You should accept the repayment, as it validates his sincerity. Even if you prefer to pick up the tab on occasion, you can do it on your next outing.

If he almost always picks up the tab, he may not feel like he has to pay you back this one time. If you're not comfortable asking him to, you can let it ride and eat the bill. But if he starts to pull this trick with any regularity, pay attention. He could simply be cheap and devious. If you're finding he tends to forget his wallet on more expensive outings, and still doesn't offer to repay you, it's a sign of a character flaw. Move on. This guy will end up costing you much more if you stay with him.

Trust your instincts. If you suspect that he's more attracted to your wallet than he is to you, you need to reevaluate the relationship. If you earn more than your partner, have inherited wealth, or descend from a highly affluent family, you'll have to be particularly careful. Your situation may be particularly attractive to The Mooch.

If The Mooch Has a Purchase on Your Heart:

There's hope if...
✳ His cash-poor state is clearly temporary.
✳ You accept that he is working for an organization (philanthropic, nonprofit, or government) where the rewards are not financial.
✳ He is as frugal with your money as he is with his own, showing fiscal restraint and no signs of taking advantage of your generosity.

✳ You take turns picking up the tab or splitting checks, and you're not always stuck with the bigger bills.

✳ He's an enthusiastic networker who is making an honest effort to advance his career.

✳ He is honest and does what he's says he's going to do, especially when it concerns paying you back or fulfilling other financial responsibilities.

Ditch him if...

✳ He pushes you too soon to mingle finances in an investment, a start-up business, or a property purchase, especially when your risk will be higher or your control will be less than his.

✳ You get the feeling that you are subsidizing his lifestyle and he's making no attempt to cover his share of expenses.

✳ He uses a financial crisis (inability to pay his rent, for example) to pressure you into letting him move in.

✳ He's too calculating about when you pay (the big bills) and when he pays (the discounts).

✳ He's interested in socializing only with people he can use for financial gain.

✳ There are any signs that he's stealing or embezzling money from you.

Profile 18:
Mr. Object-or

Y OU MEET A GUY AND conduct the ritualistic first-
date dinner. You go out for a movie next, followed
by lunch, then drinks. Then one of you invites the
other over for a home-cooked meal. The sexual tension has
been there from the start, and it isn't long before you consummate the relationship.

You're physically compatible, and the sex becomes more
than regular. Sometimes you skip the date part altogether and
spend the evening in bed. Although the sexual chemistry between you seems ideal, the emotional excitement is stalling.
You don't have a lot to talk about. You haven't met his friends,
and you aren't eager to introduce him to yours, perhaps because they may notice the two of you aren't exactly clicking.

As the relationship progresses, he takes you out less often,
with few dates scheduled in "prime time"—Friday and Saturday nights. When you do bother going to a show or sporting event, it feels like the obligatory lead-up to pillow talk.

You may have met Mr. Object-or. Unlike Mr. Rush Job,
he'll want to keep seeing you once he's slept with you. But
Mr. Object-or really only has one thing in mind when you're

together: sex. He's unwilling, unable, or uninterested in an emotional connection.

Mr. Object-or is the kind of guy who tends to segment his social life. His colleagues are for work, his buddies are for socializing, and girlfriends are for sex. He may have love in his life, from family members or close friends, but for some reason he can't open his heart to simultaneous sexual and emotional feelings, at least not with you.

He may even start up the *booty call* with you. He's out with friends or working late or just plain doing something else. He calls you up late in the evening to ask you what you're up to and whether you want company. You oblige, since you were in the mood yourself and sleeping alone doesn't seem nearly as gratifying.

The first time you permit a guy you are casually dating to do this, you're letting him know this behavior is acceptable. Congratulations, your quality girlfriend stock has just taken a nosedive!

He may even be setting you up as a future "speed dial" girl. When I was on the dating circuit, I had friends who had a host of women's phone numbers on speed dial. When they struck out late on the bar tour, they started dialing. They'd try to catch women still out and about, but they had no shame in calling them at home if their cell phones went into voice mail. Why would they be embarrassed, when many of these women acquiesced?

I can't recall even one of those women marrying a man who regularly used her for a late-night booty call. These guys turned to their speed-dial girls only when in between girlfriends or during a dry spell. The connection never turned into anything serious.

One way to prevent your relationship from getting to this point is to refuse to let your man take you for granted. Make sure that he makes plans with you in advance. Don't let him call you regularly at four p.m. to request "a quick dinner" at seven—"quick" being code for getting to the sex right after the meal! It is fine to be spontaneous once in awhile, though, especially if he keeps a busy schedule.

Note: It's a different matter if you're in a committed relationship and do things together regularly. You may arrange in advance to spend the early part of the evening with friends, then rendezvous later in the evening. My wife and I used to reserve Friday nights as friends' night before we got married and had children. We always knew that we could plan something in advance with our friends without consulting each other. We had the option of hooking up later in the evening, but we already had each other's mutual respect and the knowledge that the following night would be a real date night.

I'm not saying a guy's physical attraction to you is a bad thing. I'm just trying to make it clear that if you really want to meet a long-term prospect, you need to set some standards for him and discipline yourself. Guys aren't likely to hold back themselves, even if they later judge you (consciously or unconsciously) for being easy.

A good way to avoid finding yourself stuck with Mr. Object-or is to delay sleeping with a new man. Don't be guided by popular concepts like the "Third Date Rule," which states that if you haven't had sex by the third date, the relationship is going nowhere. *Profile 2: Mr. Rush Job* discusses why it's important to put off intimacy until you've done *The Hot Prospect Background Check.*

He may respect you for waiting and think it's a sign that he's special. You are also building up the imagination, and good things do come to those who wait. If he's really after just one thing, you'll know it, because he won't have the patience to wait.

Once you do have sex, there may be some awkwardness. You shouldn't panic and expect an immediate commitment. You may scare even a good prospect away with high expectations.

There's also the possibility a man will turn out to be Mr. Object-or anyway, even after you make him wait! A guy may love the buildup of sexual tension the delay causes, but once you consummate, all he wants to do is keep…consummating! If you're wary of this possibility, don't let your man expect sex from you every time you see each other. Mix it up, throw him off course, and see if he recovers. You don't want him coming to see you just for sex.

If, in the end, you realize that you can only connect with

your partner physically, don't let yourself get complacent. You know you want more out of a relationship. Even if you commit to this man, your inability to connect emotionally will eventually backfire.

Take the saga of a New Jersey attorney in her early thirties. She began dating an aspiring actor. She was attracted to his good looks, while he was taken in by her charm and success. Their sexual compatibility was fiery, but otherwise they had very little in common. While her career advanced, he was forced to work menial jobs, mainly because he didn't have much talent as an actor and wasn't very bright. But it took until a year after they were married for them to admit they had very little to talk about outside the bedroom. After they decided to separate, she realized she was pregnant. They divorced, but being a single mom hurt her career and her finances, as he contributes no child support.

Don't fool yourself into thinking the good sex will compensate for the lack of compatibility. It won't. If you let Mr. Object-or take up your time, you'll only despise him later for distracting you from finding the right guy.

If You Have Special Chemistry with Mr. Object-or:

There's hope if...
　✳ He continues to see you, even when you make it clear you're not ready for sex.
　✳ He schedules activities that don't always necessarily lead to bed.

177

* The sex is great, and you have a lot to talk about.
* He gives you prime-time (weekend-night) dates.
* He's introducing you to his friends, colleagues, and family, signs that he respects you.
* He's genuinely interested in you, not just having sex with you.

Ditch him if...
* He shows no interest in anything about you but sex.
* When you put the breaks on intimacy, he loses interest.
* Once you've slept with him, he becomes less enthusiastic about scheduling activities and going out in public with you.
* He's keeping you away from his social circle.
* You're not interested in bringing him into your social circle.
* You have nothing to talk about outside the bedroom.

Profile 19:
Mr. Twisted, Sister!

●●●●●●●●●●●●●●●●●

P ART OF ROMANCE IS FINDING a guy who can push your hot buttons, and even discover some you didn't know existed. He may take you into a new realm sexually, with lots of adventurous experimentation. You may engage in activities that one might consider less than conventional.

There's not necessarily anything wrong with this. A good amount of sexual variation occurs behind closed doors. It's essentially a personal matter, especially if the participants are discreet.

Some women feel like they can really be themselves only with Mr. Twisted. He sets them free. With him they can enjoy a romance with fewer traditional expectations and hang-ups.

But many women don't travel down this deviated path quite so readily. So before we get too wrapped up in an "anything goes" mentality, I need to emphasize one important factor:

Don't do anything you're not comfortable doing for his sake, or you'll regret it.

That means, don't get kinky because you're simply try-ing to satisfy his sexual appetite, or he's convinced you that it's cool. Don't go wild because you need to prove you're not uptight. Don't agree to something you're unsure about be-cause you're afraid you'll lose your man. Your self-esteem and possibly your reputation should be higher priorities than his deviant desires. If he does leave, that means he wasn't worth a moment more of your time, in the sack or outside the bedroom.

Once you accept this basic advice, consider some ad-ditional concerns:

Are you being filmed? Even if you think you trust this guy, you don't want to be the featured actress on an X-rated YouTube or home video.

Are certain activities becoming essential to your sexual plea-sure, or his? You or your partner may find that you need a porn flick, gadget, costume, or a third person to enjoy sex. Does it bother you if you can't get back to basics, particu-larly if that's your preference?

During my single days, a rather charismatic and gregari-ous guy routinely had his way with women. He could con-vince them to do almost anything. He normally would ply them with alcohol. This man had his dates disrobing in pub-lic, making love on display, going to underground sex clubs, and even introducing guy friends or other women into the mix. I don't recall any of these women sticking around very long. Most of them realized they had been used and possibly abused, and they were not very proud of the behavior into which they'd been lured.

Are you practicing safe sex? No outré behavior is worth getting an STD or an unplanned pregnancy.

How will you feel the next day? You may be vulnerable, lonely, depressed, drunk, high, on the "rebound," or simply wild right now, but what will you think of yourself in the morning? Will you want Mr. Twisted to stay for another round of fun, or will you cringe at the sight of him? Is there a chance you will lose respect for each other?

Are other women involved? If you and your man have invited another woman into your bed, he may never leave you alone with a cute girlfriend again. It's hard enough to trust you not to sleep with other men, but now you've doubled the landscape of concern.

I know a man who was ecstatic to find that his new girlfriend liked to invite other women to bed with them, fulfilling his raciest fantasies. After they got married, though, he wasn't happy to learn she still enjoyed other women—even when he wasn't invited. The marriage didn't last long.

Are several others involved? Swinging can be a blast for some couples, but keep in mind that it's very hard to keep secrets when you're wife-swapping, going to key parties, or indulging in any other behavior that isn't just between the two of you.

A woman I know had to break ties with her entire social circle after engaging in a ménage à trois on the suggestion of a man she was dating. She's still worried the story will leak to new prospects, further damaging her reputation.

Speaking of which:

Are you worried about being judged? Some women want to be accepted no matter what they did in their past, figuring that any guy who judges them isn't worth it. Many men will judge them, though, as I've discussed. If you want to be available to men who might be uncomfortable with the far-out tricks you've tried, then proceed with Mr. Twisted with caution.

You may be caught up in the moment with Mr. Twisted, but remember: A few moments don't make your life. A little caution and foresight now will prevent later regrets. Always take the time to look inside yourself and ask: Is this really me? Will I truly enjoy what I'm about to do, not just now, but tomorrow and in the future?

If You're Swinging with Mr. Twisted, Sister!

There's hope if...
* You genuinely enjoy your sex life with him.
* You feel free to initiate new activities and aren't just following his lead all the time.
* You indulge in a healthy mix of erotic adventures and more traditional lovemaking.

✳ You feel safe and cared for, not just his "wild thing."

✳ Your self-esteem has improved because you feel like you can truly be yourself in his company.

✳ He's helped you release prior inhibitions.

Ditch him if...

✳ You're uncomfortable with his sexual demands.

✳ He insists on documenting your adventures in photographs and on video, despite your protests.

✳ You feel under pressure to do what he says in order to maintain the relationship.

✳ He pushes you to engage in activities that are uncomfortable, unsafe, or even painful.

✳ He violates your trust by gossiping about you or "swinging" without your consent.

✳ You feel that you cannot offer enough to satisfy his sexual desires and fear he'll be unfaithful because of it.

Profile 20:
Mr. Noncomittal

A CERTAIN GENTLEMAN LIKED TO PLAY the field throughout his twenties and thirties. He had two serious girlfriends into his early twenties. The first was his high school sweetheart. They drifted apart during college, recognizing they had very different personal and professional goals. The second one had a nervous breakdown when he made a career move that relocated him across the country. After this painful emotional encounter, he vowed not to get serious for some time. He decided career, world travel, and having fun would come first.

He dated several gals at a time, juggling names and schedules along with demanding career obligations and frequent business and vacation travel. Every once in a while, a relationship might become semi-serious or even exclusive, but most of the time he enjoyed the life of an eligible bachelor.

When he did get involved with someone romantically, he'd eventually get fed up with something about her and end it. None of the relationships felt like long-term prospects, at least not to him. It became very easy to identify Ms. Wrong, but for quite some time, no one passed his mental checklist for Mrs. Right!

This guy held out through his twenties, his thirties, and the big four-oh birthday, shaking off questions from family and friends about when he was going to settle down.

At this point, you may be shaking your head, thinking, I know that guy. He isn't going to settle down, not ever. He's one of those guys who can't commit.

Well, you do know this guy, in a way. He's me.

And you're wrong about him. I got married at age forty-two. I dated the woman who is now my wife on and off for several years. When she told me she needed a commitment beyond casual dating after the third year, I realized she was the best woman I had ever met and I couldn't let her go. I was ready to share my life. With her, I didn't need to make too many compromises to do so.

Most men don't commit for the same reason I didn't commit when I was a bachelor:

A. They're not ready, or
B. You're not the right person.

For more details on A, you may want to review the section *"He's Truly Ready for Marriage When…"* in the introduction to this book.

Obviously, the "finding the right person" part is trickier. For me, it was about finding the right match physically, intellectually, and emotionally and having overlapping personal and professional goals. Most important, we both wanted kids fairly soon. Timing was critical. I clearly wasn't ready for a wife or a family ten or possibly even five years earlier. In the end, you have to accept that if your man doesn't think you're the right person, he's not going to marry you, no matter how long you've been together.

Many women push for a commitment of exclusivity or even marriage too soon in a relationship. Realize that, from a guy's perspective, the moment you initiate The Big Relationship Talk is the moment he thinks, "The party has officially ended!" His carefree lifestyle with you is coming to an end. He may need to step back and reevaluate. He may be willing to move forward with an initial promise not to date anyone else, though that doesn't mean he won't balk at a deeper commitment (moving in together, engagement, marriage, or children) later.

Don't have unrealistic expectations. If you told me that you were intimate with a man within a month of dating and then wanted his commitment for exclusivity after he'd been single for thirty-plus years, I'd say that you may have been pushing him too quickly. For a man, sex doesn't necessarily equal a relationship.

My advice is that you should not push for an initial commitment of exclusivity until there's a natural bilateral connection. If you are seeing someone quite regularly, have a physical relationship, and are not comfortable with him sleeping with others, then you need to tell him. Guys often require a bit more space, though. You don't want to push him prematurely, but you also need to establish guidelines that protect you physically and emotionally.

Note: The concept of "seeing someone quite regularly" can vary from couple to couple. If either of you works long hours, is responsible for children, has night hours at work or school, or has a heavy travel schedule, you may get together relatively infrequently (weekends only, for example). For others, regular contact may be almost daily, with sleepovers and phone conversations. Your lives are entwined and you make plans around each other's schedules.

By this point, you should also be able to answer all the questions on the *Dating Litmus Test* and get an acceptable score (see Part One).

Women often get caught up in the whirlwind of the early days of romance, thinking this relationship is The One, before they really get the facts about a guy. But let me ask you this. Would you really want to stop dating other guys for a man who:

• Doesn't want kids, when you know you do?
• Wants to settle down in his hometown in Minnesota, when you want to live in a warm climate or possibly overseas for a spell?
• Hasn't proven to be trustworthy?

If he's the one who's refusing to be exclusive, despite a decent score on the Dating Litmus Test and sufficient time to decide, you can issue the "trade me or play me" ultimatum. Some guys who may hedge on initiating a commitment themselves respond well when presented with the alternative: not having you in their life! I certainly did, when the time and person were right.

You should be respectful and time sensitive on how you address this topic. I wouldn't suggest initiating this conversation in front of other people or during a time of extreme duress for him at work.

Do some footwork in advance. It is fair to ask him what his expectations are for a long-term relationship or what his personal timetables are for settling down and having a family. If his timetable and yours don't come close to coinciding, then you need to know that even if this guy might some day commit, for your purposes, he's Mr. Wrong.

If he trades you, you may be sad or feel you've pressed your luck. But remember that it's better you know now and aren't going to be wasting any more time.

The exclusivity agreement is the first of several levels of commitment. It's in many ways the easiest—men who may readily stop dating other women may balk at the far more serious steps of moving in together or marriage. Retake the Dating Litmus Test to see whether his score is going up or down before broaching any of these subsequent

Big Relationship Talk queries:

- Do you love me?
- Should we move in together?
- Should we get married?
- Are you open to having children together?

At this point, you may be looking for some specific guidance on timetables. It's not a simple matter. Every circumstance is unique. A few examples:

- If you are thirty-five, don't have children, and want a family, you shouldn't be dating a man for more than six months who doesn't score high on the Dating Litmus Test. If he doesn't want children, don't go beyond casual dating status with him.
- If you are twenty-five, involved with a guy for three years who is in medical or law school or in the early stages of his own career, and he isn't ready to settle down, be patient but certainly keep your options open. Pursue your own career, in case his bright future doesn't include you!
- If you are in your thirties or older and don't plan to have any (or additional) children, you can be far more patient. It's fine to be with a man for a few years and take your time with intermediate steps—exclusivity, cohabitation—before considering marriage, if desired.

If the guy earns your trust and respect and has always done what he said he was going to do, then you should give him some slack. He just needs to come to the same conclusion that you have. If he isn't moving fast enough to suit your needs, you may be justified in presenting him with the "play me or trade me" ultimatum.

No matter what, you need to accept the situation when your man tells you he doesn't want to move forward to a deeper level of commitment. He may not be ready to break up with you, but if he tells you he doesn't want to marry you and you want to get married, consider yourself fully informed. Don't assume he will change his mind. You may throw away years of your life waiting. Move on.

All the time and space in the world won't fix the guys out there who do have serious commitment problems or character flaws. You've read about them already in a number of the profiles. They drive relationships into the ground by cheating, lying, stealing, manipulating, and other tactics, intentional or otherwise.

The most seductive type of Mr. Noncomittal is The Playboy. He's that foxy man everyone knows and half the girls in town have dated. He has no plans to settle down, not even for a night, much less a lifetime!

The Playboy is:

✳ Good-looking, stylish, and popular with both women and men

✳ Connected with the en vogue social networks

✳ Full of mystique, because so many women court him yet no one can have him

✳ So egotistical that one woman cannot satisfy his appetite

✳ Used to getting his way with women

✳ Overconfident and downright cocky or snobbish

✳ Concerned with satisfying his own selfish interests

✳ Not highly respectful of women in general

✳ Dating and sleeping with multiple partners at the same time

✳ Bent on remaining unengaged during "prime times" so he can hunt for new dates

✳ Prone to confuse details, forgetting which professions, likes and dislikes, schedules, and even names belong to which women

✳ Unreliable as a colleague, friend, and lover

✳ Apt to blow you off at the last moment for a better offer

✳ A risk for sexually transmitted diseases

✳ Likely to lie to, deceive, or openly cheat on you

Know what you are getting yourself in for. If you want to have fun with The Playboy, protect yourself physically and emotionally. But if you want more, this guy is not a good option, at least not now. He may one day settle down, but you shouldn't wait in the wings for him.

There are also the men who are truly damaged goods, with difficult broken marriages, traumatic childhoods, or bad parents as role models for relationships (See Profile 10: Mr. Heavy Baggage). No matter how much sympathy you may feel for them, you may not be able to prevent them from acting out in ways that sabotage your relationship, causing his Dating Litmus Test score to quickly plummet.

No matter why men with these types of commitment phobias do what they do, ultimately their issues lead you right back to the two main reasons men don't commit: He's either not ready or you're not the right person. He may never be ready. He may never find the right person. That's his problem. You should part ways as soon as possible so it's no longer your problem, too.

If You Want to Settle Down with Mr. Noncommittal:

There's hope if...
＊ He approaches big commitment decisions as emotional challenges that take serious time and thought.
＊ He treats you with love and respect as he sorts through major decisions, sensitized to your personal requirements.

✳ He is a devoted son, brother, or friend.

✳ Though he's been divorced or burned emotionally, he treats it as a learning experience, not as an excuse to avoid commitment.

✳ Though he's a longtime bachelor, he makes it clear that he's not averse to marriage or raising a family.

✳ He communicates his intentions openly and clearly, providing you with a timeline that he can live with.

Ditch him if...

✳ "Needing a little time" to decide on a commitment means additional years and repeated delays.

✳ He exploits your vulnerability as a woman who wants him to commit by taking advantage of you financially, emotionally, or sexually.

✳ You are never considered a top priority.

✳ He shows no signs of being committed to anyone in his life.

✳ His timeline for making a decision or commitment is constantly being delayed for reasons that don't make sense.

✳ He tells you he never wants to fall in love, live with someone, get married, or have children (Don't take these statements lightly!).

PART THREE

Getting Rid of Mr. Wrong and Starting Over

Women's Rationales
for Not Exiting Bad
Relationships

YOU'VE TAKEN THE DATING LITMUS Test several
times. Your score started out weak and only got
worse. You've read through the profiles and found
one that fits your man. You may have even found two or
more, making him the kind of guy I like to call Mr. Double-
Trouble! In any case, this fellow's attributes fall solidly into
the "ditch him if" category.

The writing is on the wall. Actually, it's a flashing, ten-
foot-tall neon sign over the highway of your life: DITCH
HIM!

So why can't you bring yourself to do it?

After seven years of life coaching, Gretchen Sunderland
has heard the phrase "But I just can't leave him!" dozens
of times. She's watched too many women throw away too
much precious time with Mr. Wrong.

Perhaps one of her observations will sound familiar to
you.

Fear: "No one else will ever want me."

Arrogance: "No one knows him like I do. I can change him."

Sex: "It's not going to be this good with anyone else."

Time: "I've already invested so much in this relationship."

Loneliness: "I don't want to be alone."

Ignorance: "Men are all pretty much like him, aren't they?"

Effort: "I'd have to work too hard (lose weight, get a makeover, end addictions, rebuild social networks) to get a better one."

Defensiveness: "You just don't know all his good qualities."

As women decide whether to end a relationship, they often struggle with a sense of failure. They think their parents, friends, or co-workers will shake their heads and judge them for not being able to hold on to a man.

I'd like to suggest another way of thinking about ditching Mr. Wrong: *Every relationship that doesn't work out prepares you for finding Mr. Right.*

You'll learn a lot about yourself and what you want in a relationship by dating different men. You'll find out more about your own likes, dislikes, and emotional hot buttons. You'll discover what's physically appealing to you, what hobbies you want to share, and what kind of life you want to have. Your dating years provide a hands-on educational process that almost everyone goes through, except people who marry their first sweetheart or those whose culture requires them to enter an arranged marriage.

None of the above rationales is enough to justify staying with a man who is clearly Mr. Wrong. But it's understandable if you're willing to accept a less-than-perfect relationship because you're growing older and running out of time to start a family. He may score only a B, but that's far better than the Cs and Ds you've been with in the past.

Getting Rid Of Mr. Wrong in Ten Easy Steps

✳ **Step One: Be Positive.**

You've probably shared some special and intimate moments with this man. So, if at all possible, it's best to end the relationship on amiable terms. You'll feel better about yourself and you'll part ways in a better state of mind. The worst breakups occur when both parties exacerbate the pain with poor behavior.

✳ **Step Two: Set a Timeline.**

The sooner you accept the "officially broken up" status, the better. If you are living together, you need to come up with a firm deadline (no more than a few weeks) for making separate living arrangements.

✳ **Step Three: End the Physical Connection.**

If you haven't gotten to moving-out day yet, you still need to sleep separately. So many couples get back together because they resume their sexual relationship. If the temptation is too strong, find a friend's couch to sleep on.

✳ **Step Four: Don't Flaunt the New Guy**

Don't bring a third party into the equation. If you've already started to date, that's fine, but avoid exposing your ex to your new life. If your partner cheated on you, you may be tempted to pay him back, but you are only demeaning yourself by stooping to this level. Treat your ex the way you would like to be treated.

✳ Step Five: Don't Bad-Talk Him.

Even if you're justifiably upset at his philandering, deceptions, or other unacceptable behavior, confide only in close family members and best friends. Don't make public the sordid details of your breakup. Spreading dirt about your ex will keep you from getting over the relationship. It can also backfire and make you look bad.

✳ Step Six: Agree on Property.

Be fair. Ask yourselves, who brought what into the relationship? If he paid for everything, you may be at his mercy. He owns what he purchased. If you shared costs, establish need versus want. With animals, consider who had the pet first, who was the "primary caretaker," and where the pet would enjoy a better standard of living. If children are involved, this is a whole other issue. The best interests of the children come first. You may need to seek legal counsel.

✳ Step Seven: Agree on the Division of Assets.

Divvy up bank accounts and investments properly and completely. Do not continue to share a financial connection. If you purchased property together, you either must buy your ex out, let him buy you out, or liquidate the asset and split the proceeds fairly.

✳ Step Eight: End Privileges.

Don't swim in his pool. Don't let yourself into his apartment to use the bathroom whenever you're in the neighborhood. Don't run up a balance on his credit card. Taking advantage of these pre-breakup perks can range from territorial (you're checking up on him) to unfair to illegal.

✳ Step Nine: Avoid Attorneys.

Lawyer fees range from $150 to $350 an hour, billable in quarter-hour increments. Attorneys operate with a win–loss mentality. They'll advise you to go after the maximum possible, knowing that compromises will occur. This can transform what could be an agreeable breakup into a war.

✳ Step Ten: Forgive Yourself.

You may not have been perfect, but relationships are really tough! Not many of them succeed. Nearly half of all marriages end in divorce. An even higher percentage of premarital relationships won't last, but that doesn't mean the individuals in them are failures.

Once you've done the deed and left him, avoid breakup remorse. You may experience regret, be haunted by memories from a happier time, and be tempted to reconcile. Don't! You didn't do all that work for nothing.

You may also be suffering from shaky confidence. Use this feeling of insecurity as a motivating force for self-improvement.

Getting Back Into the Game

Now that you've made the break, it's time to think about dating again. You've learned a lot already about how to spot Mr. Wrong. But how should you act when you're looking for Mr. Right?

Dating Protocol

✳ Q: How quickly should I call, text message, or e-mail him back?

✳ A: In the same amount of time that you would want him to respond to you! Don't keep him waiting just to try to establish the upper hand.

✳ Q: Do I let the call go into voice mail, even though I know it's him?

✳ A: If you're available and he's phoning at a reasonable hour, take the call. If you're too busy or rushed or he's calling too late or too early, return the call later.

✳ Q: Do I make him repeat his attempts to contact me?

✳ A: You shouldn't. But if for some reason you didn't return his call within a reasonable amount of time and you are still interested, be honest, sincere, and apologetic.

✳ Q: Will I appear too eager if I tell him that I want to see him again soon?

✳ A: Possibly. If he takes the initiative to ask you out,

he's showing interest. Be patient. You want him to know that you have other things going on in your life.

⁕ Q: How much interest should I demonstrate?

⁕ A: You don't want to be overly enthusiastic initially. He may take advantage of you. If he's a longtime bachelor, your forwardness may even scare him off.

⁕ Q: Do I give up "prime time" (weekends) yet for dates?

⁕ A: Yes. If he's willing to do so, you should as well.

⁕ Q: When I'm dolling up for a first date with a man, should I dress in a conservative or sexy manner?

⁕ A: Dress appropriately for the activity and leave as much to the imagination as possible.

⁕ Q: How do I choose between two men who are interested in me?

⁕ A: Go on a Résumé Date (or several) with each and determine who comes out ahead. There is nothing better than having options and being able to compare.

⁕ Q: How do I avoid giving up the upper hand without letting him think or know that he is in control?

⁕ A: Be yourself and demonstrate reasons why he would want to keep seeing you. The worst thing is to pretend you are something you are clearly not.

⁕ Q: When is it appropriate to invite him back to my place or accept an invitation to his abode?

⁕ A: Once you feel comfortable and safe with him.

⁕ Q: If we go into private quarters, does this send the message that I'm available for intimacy?

⁕ A: Not if you clarify that is not your intent. Men typically follow a woman's lead. But if given the chance, they will try to "push all the right buttons" to move the relationship toward sex.

✳ Q: Will a guy's expectations change after we've been intimate?

✳ A: Not usually. It depends on whether he's looking for Mrs. Right or just casually dating. Don't expect him to automatically want to be exclusive after you've slept together.

✳ Q: When do I bring a new man to meet friends, family, or colleagues?

✳ A: Once you are confident he will not embarrass you and are comfortable enough with him to introduce him to others as a friend or boyfriend.

✳ Q: At what point are we classified as an exclusive "boyfriend and girlfriend" couple?

✳ A: This transformation can happen naturally, but more frequently it's after you've had The Talk and established your official status.

The Eligible Bachelorette Checklist

As you take your first steps back into the singles scene, you may want to consider ways you can become a better candidate to attract a suitable mate.

From a man's perspective, here are some areas to hone in on:

✳ **Current affairs:** Keep up with what's going on in the news and educate yourself on international affairs, economics, trends, politics, culture, and some major or local sports.

✳ **Good character:** Get your act together. Guys definitely are attracted to physical characteristics first, but when they start shopping for a wife, their antennas tune in to more substantial issues:
  • Are you reliable or flakey?
  • Can you be depended upon to help out or contribute?
  • Are you a taker or a giver?
  • Can you be trusted?
  • Are you organized? (finances, personal schedule)
  • Are you independent, or is someone (such as family or an old boyfriend) supporting you until the next "meal ticket" comes along?

✳ **Physical fitness:** If you've let yourself go, it's a good time to get in shape.

✳ **Domesticity:** Take care of your own household. When I was dating, I once went into a woman's home and the relationship was over before it started. Dirty dishes in the sink, disgusting bathrooms, and laundry scattered on the floor are all turn-offs.

✳ **Computer literacy:** In this day and age, being technology savvy is critical for communicating and getting information, both in professional situations and on matters of health, child care, home improvement, entertainment, and other aspects of family life.

✳ **Social life:** Men have disdain for women that have a 100 percent emotional dependency on them. They like to escape periodically to bond with the boys, focus on their work, or recharge, and it's good if you have friends and family who support you and provide you with your own getaway opportunities.

✳ **Conflict resolution:** If you're always unhappy and complaining about your relationships with co-workers, family, and friends, chances are that you'll be equally miserable with a significant other.

✳ **Children:** If you want to have children, get some experience with them. Be an involved aunt or friend to the kids in your life. Guys who want a family look for maternal characteristics in women they date.

✳ **Telephone etiquette:** Don't try to keep interested men on the phone too long, or call them at odd hours. A woman who can't keep herself from needlessly bothering a man when he's at work or with his friends is extremely annoying.

✳ **Sexuality:** Now that you're looking for a life partner, you should be more cautious about how many men you sleep with. Many men don't want woman with an overly promiscuous track record as a wife. You don't need to be a virgin, but show some restraint.

✳ **Bad habits:** Smoking is one of those "deal breakers," unless you're looking for another smoker. Same goes with drinking or substance abuse. Even if you're not an alcoholic or a drug addict, avoid getting smashed, especially in public. You're likely to behave foolishly.

✳ **Tune up:** Make sure you don't have bad teeth, a real turn-off, and that you're well groomed. Cosmetic surgery may be going too far. Consider it only if it's really required.

✳ **Finances:** Don't be financially needy. I know guys who've moved in with a woman and found that the first thing they had to do was pay off her credit cards. Then they helped with her car payments and co-signed her mortgage. If men are going to have to pay for sex, they can go the professional route and limit their losses.

Now that you've spruced yourself up, you're ready to meet new men. How many stories have you heard from your friends about meeting Mr. Right in a bar, nightclub, or someplace else even more decadent? Probably not very many. So where should you go to meet a quality guy? Start with attending activities you already enjoy, and exploring new areas where there's a decent likelihood of finding a guy with a strong character and common interests.

Consider:

⁕ **House parties:** The hosts and their friends can help you prescreen men they already know.

⁕ **Health clubs:** Here you can network with presumably healthy people, and most facilities have great social activities.

⁕ **Sporting events:** The male-to-female ratio will be ideal, and guys will be curious about a woman who's into sports.

⁕ **Church or synagogue:** In addition to regular services, houses of worship frequently sponsor singles events—the perfect opportunity to find someone who shares your faith.

⁕ **Festivals:** Mingle at cultural events celebrating local wine, art, or music, often held at downtown locations.

⁕ **Holiday and special-occasion parties:** Dress up in your seasonal best and spread some cheer!

⁕ **Office social events:** I suggest getting invited to activities at your friends' companies, since dating at your own workplace may be risky.

⁕ **Sports teams** (e.g., co-ed volleyball or softball) **or leagues** (e.g., tennis, golf): Have fun, stay in shape, and meet men with whom you already have something in common.

⁕ **Volunteer work or community organizations:** Meet someone good by doing good for a cause in which you both believe.

These lists may seem overwhelming. Don't take on too much at once, and don't get discouraged. Do not, I repeat, *do not* romanticize your former relationship with Mr. Wrong, just because it was safer than being "out there" again. And don't go back to him!

There are a lot of potential Mr. Rights out there. The sooner you dispose of the poor prospects, the faster you position yourself to meet a great catch. I'm not saying that finding the right guy is the only way you can find happiness, but the converse is a certainty: Being with the wrong guy guarantees that you will be unhappy!

Stop permitting the Mr. Wrongs of the world to distract you from meeting good candidates. The only way these mismatches can be useful to you now is as part of your learning process to find out what truly matters to you in a lifelong partner.

Picking Mr. Right may be the most important decision of your entire life and beyond. Think of yourself as the bottom of your future family tree. The man you spend your life with will have an impact on every single branch that sprouts for generations: your children, their spouses, their children, and so on.

Ditching your Mr. Wrong isn't really about ending something. It's about giving you the opportunity for a new beginning. Now that you know how to leave a bad relationship and spot Mr. Wrong from a mile away, you're free to open your life and your heart to meeting Mr. Right.

Ditching

When I was a girl, love had a different meaning.
It was never a priority to do a detailed screening.
Character wasn't something that I thought a lot about.
As long as he was fun, he could take me out.

Steve's so good-looking, but like a dog in heat.
A mysterious man, he was like to be a cheat.
Brian's goal was clear: to rush me into the sack.
I don't mind since he's cute, but as for love, there's a lack.

I want a festive wedding and a lovely gown,
Would like to have children, but time's winding down.
I've squandered many years with guys who didn't really care,
Working out and starving, even bleaching my dark hair.

Frank wined and dined me at all the fancy places.
I learned he was married, I should have seen the traces.
Richard is intellectual yet bores me to tears.
He acts like a professor, validating all my fears.

I should have researched these candidates better,
Believed the writings in an old girlfriend's letter.
These men couldn't be trusted with money or with fame.
The excuses they provided were perpetually quite lame.

Chorus 1

I just wanna be held, have someone to love.
Is that too much to ask from the powers above?
I'd like a little bit cute and a lot of fun,
I'd be happier than opposed to having no one.

Give me a guy with wealth, not one who's poor,
But the last thing I want is a guy who's a bore!
One day I feel great, while the next I'm quite sad.
I'll compromise standards 'cause he can't be that bad.

One makes me laugh and another is so sly.
Can't I get any luck picking the right guy?
I primp and search and try to take chances
Yet I still feel like a failure in lasting romances!

I need to ditch the weak ones before things go wrong.
Ascertaining which decisions are taking too long,
Avoiding distractions or external forces,
I'll learn faster how to cut short my losses.

Since I was young, I believed the fairy tale.
Dreamed Prince Charming would be arriving without fail.
He'd rescue me from dreary times living all alone.
He'd make me forget all the sorrow I've known.

Jerry foots the bills, I don't pay a dime.
He doesn't take me seriously, it's quite a crime.
Brad is artistic. I find it a shame
He can't afford rent, no one else is to blame.

I'm in my thirties, most friends have now been wed.
I spend many nights solo, lying chilly in bed,
Wanting a husband and kids to share my love.
Misery may be destiny without help from above.

John loves to argue, which leads to a fight.
Habitual debating has me constantly uptight.
Aaron likes to control, causing me some concern.
Dominates my schedule. When will I ever learn?

I had so many choices, how could I then decide?
Others made selections and have lives full of pride.
I was young and attractive, so very much stronger.
How long must I wait? I don't have much longer.

Chorus 2

I'd like to have fun and find some real romance,
Avoiding guys who just want to get into my pants.
I need someone honest and makes an admission,
Not trying to spar and beat me into submission.

Any handsome guys around with businesses intact?
Or are most of them losers, and is that a fact?
When will I learn to toss bad prospects aside?
The rules have now changed, I need to abide.

At the end of the day, what will it now cost
To date so many men whose futures are lost?
I thought we had promise, he sure told me so.
Since losing free lodging, where can I now go?

I gotta ditch Mr. Wrong before life goes awry.
I promised if he'd leave, I wouldn't even cry.
Gotta find the right guy to avoid dating disaster.
I dearly want to live happily ever after.

I long for someone special, I search for a mate.
I don't want to accept being single as my fate.
I spent so many years chasing candidates away.
Procrastination resulted in this highly dreadful day!

Mark's career has arrived, albeit quite late.
It seems unfair that he's now overweight!
David's real nice, but indulged himself too long.
He's paying the price, a likely Mr. Wrong.

At first he was fit and he wasn't so lazy.
Now his future is bleak and somewhat hazy.
Some guys may find some respectable work,
Then hit the bottle hard, turning into a jerk.

Ron was mature and established in his game.
A pity he's old, I find his stories are lame.
Danny is spry, a boy toy, a hunk.
Too bad younger guys endure so much career funk.

One was too young and the last was too old.
How long can I wait for my life to unfold?
The decision's for life, and I know he won't change.
Was life so great that I can't rearrange?

{Repeat Chorus 1}

I've made real effort, and I'll retake the test.
But how do I know which guy will work best?
We've moved in together but constantly clash.
Do I toss him out quick, with today's bag of trash?

Mike is sincere, someone who can confide.
He has great ambition, but can he provide?
Kenneth has ADD, simply can't pay attention.
Not looking for love, just the latest invention.

He seems really sweet, his heart's in the right place.
Too bad in the daytime, I can't look at his face!
He has all these bad habits, do I settle for less?
I must face the fact: His life is a mess.

Bobby can't make decisions without Mom's consent.
I'm sure when he leaves, he will truly resent.
Tony restarted so often, it's tough to keep track.
Can he keep up with the rest of the pack?

I tried really hard, had a guy out on loan.
She wanted him back, now I must find my own.
The man I initially thought could be a good fit
Has me utterly convinced it is high time to split.

{Repeat Chorus 2}

A guy with presence, a real sense of style.
I tried making plans, I'll be waiting awhile.
His respectable career, most gals would like that,
But his ego is so swelled he needs a much larger hat.

Joey's so handsome, a total heartthrob.
Too bad he's a mooch who can't hold down a job!
Eric's playful at night and keeps me amused.
Then mornings arrive, and I find I'm confused.

He lacks any talent, is professionally inept.
He squandered his money, none of it was kept.
Guys have their vices, a gal can't compete.
Finding the right package is truly a feat!

Jeff's lots of fun, and he seems within range,
But his bedroom manner is quite awfully strange.
Nick could be the one, but he was single so long
It begs the real question, could something be wrong?

One is distracted, expecting near perfection,
Not ready just to settle, or make a final selection.
He makes a lasting impression, but will he treat you right?
Sick of this game altogether, you want to end this plight!

{Repeat Chorus 1}

About the Author

Nicholas Aretakis lived the life of a successful high-tech executive and single man of means until the age of 42, when he met and married Ms. Right. Among his observations during his time as a serial dater: Women will apply more due diligence purchasing an automobile or selecting a handbag than choosing a potential life-long partner.

With dual degrees in mathematics and electrical engineering, Aretakis now applies his analytical reasoning skills to a highly controversial subject: How to help smart single women save time and heartbreak by learning shortcuts to identifying prospective husbands. He has tapped the knowledge and research of esteemed relationship experts to validate his conclusions, and translates these findings into proactive, logical steps for selecting a suitable mate.

Aretakis is the author of a previous book, *No More Ramen: The 20-Something's Real World Survival Guide* (www.NoMoreRamenOnline.com), and has a family-run business that offers humane solutions for walking your dog, (www.ezleash.com). Aretakis and his wife, Ginger, live in Scottsdale, Arizona, and Saratoga Springs, New York, with their two little girls, Ella and Sophia, and two Jack Russell terriers.